Are Word *of* Faith Televangelists Misleading Millions?

Testing dozens of Word-Faith teachings from over 20 televangelists and authors with Scripture

Danny Frigulti

Bible Version used:

Scripture used is from the King James Version, Thomas Nelson, 1970.

Dedication

This book is dedicated to the real Jesus of the Bible for the purpose of reinforcing His true identity. Many have crept in (Jude 4) as grievous wolves speaking perverse things (Acts 20:29-30) about His Name and His blood atonement. It is also dedicated to the faithful in the past, those in the present, and in the future who have known, do know, and will know the biblical Jesus preached by the apostles.

Acknowledgements

Special thanks to Jaymes and Andy for helping with proofing and editing, Chuck with cover design, Larry with website help, and the people in my Bible studies. Most of all, thank you my Lord Jesus for strengthening me to finish this to glorify You and help Your people.

ISBN – 13: 978-1541102804

ISBN – 10: 1541102800

Author's website is www.dannyfrigulti.com

This book can be ordered from Create Space at:

https://www.createspace.com/6792780

Table of Contents

A Prophetic Warning from Scripture

In 2 Timothy 4:1-5, the apostle Paul reminded Timothy of a serious, impending problem that would penetrate the Body of Christ. Through Paul, the Holy Spirit foretold there was a time coming when the problem of false doctrine would lure believers (?) to turn away from truth (sound doctrine). It happened in the first century (Judaizers and Gnostic false doctrines about Jesus), and it's happening today from false Word-Faith doctrincs. Let's learn from these verses.

> I charge thee therefore before God, and the Lord Jesus Christ, Who shall judge the quick and the dead at His appearing and His kingdom: Preach the word; be instant in season, out of season; reprove, rebuke, exhort, with all long-suffering and doctrine. For the time will come when they will not endure sound doctrine; but after their own lusts shall they heap to themselves teachers, having itching ears; And they shall turn away their ears from the truth, and shall be turned unto fables. But watch thou in all things, endure afflictions, do the work of an evangelist, make full proof of thy ministry.

All who claim to be Christians must heed Paul's first century warning, because today we have a bigger spiritual problem. Some Christians no longer desire sound doctrine, and are leaving true Gospel preaching churches. They lust after faith teachers who present *another* version of faith doctrines for seeking gain, rather than seeking godliness.

Note: When this book was printed, all the web sources were still posted as quoted in this book. If at some time a website is removed, you can go online and find verifiable information on the topic for further study, or typing in the author's name and article that was quoted should take you to where it was originally found.

Opening Comments

For the last twenty years, there has been an increase on "Health and Wealth" messages throughout worldwide Christian television. Often, you can find various faith-emphasizing preachers trying to convince the viewers that it is God's will for all Christians to "prosper, be in good health, and receive healing from Jesus." Such ministers declare if you place faith in God's Word (specific Bible verses) that mention health and wealth, then according to your faith you will receive what your faith desires. These misled media messengers often cite Romans 10:8 where it says, "the word of faith, which we preach" to define themselves as Word of Faith or Word-Faith believers.

Word of Faith believers teach that Christ's blood sacrifice on the cross was for the forgiveness of our sins, and also guarantees physical healing and financial prosperity. Some teach this gospel as the three-fold gospel of redemption. This threefold redemption belief will be tested *thoroughly* with Scripture later in this book to verify *if* the Word of Faith gospel is the Gospel Jesus wanted preached. In Galatians 1:6-9, Paul warned Christians about the serious consequences of believing in "another gospel." He said only one Gospel was the true Gospel and *any other gospel* was accursed, and Paul received the Gospel by direct revelation from Jesus (verses 11-12).

We will look carefully at their dogmatic teachings on healing, prosperity, sickness, faith, positive confession, creative visualization, quantum faith, and other controversial biblical topics they promote. There are true and sound doctrines taught in the worldwide Word of Faith movement. However, the focus will be on exposing *false* Word-Faith doctrinal beliefs, because millions of people around the world are misled and snared by false faith teachings. When compared to Scripture throughout this book, you will see with your eyes and know

1

in your mind and heart that the core of Word of Faith teachings were not taught by the real Jesus and His apostles.

My study of what is called the "Worldwide Faith Movement," "Word of Faith," "Word-Faith," or "Faith Movement" is the result of more than thirty years of study, prayer, television observation, and discussions with Christians. During my lengthy study I have read dozens of books and booklets totaling thousands of pages written by various faith teachers, positive confession advocates, faith healers, prosperity preachers, and their former followers.

Some false doctrines exposed in this book are from men who have passed away, but their deceptive teachings live on daily in the lives of misled millions. Such men are E. W. Kenyon (1867-1948), F. F. Bosworth (1877-1958), Kenneth E. Hagin (1917-2003), T. L. Osborn (1923-2013), and Charles Capps (1934-2014). The faith preaching televangelists continue to cite these deceased ministers/authors as authoritative by using some of their previous teachings, and selling their materials. To complicate discernment between truth and error, the new breed of false faith televangelists has *added more* corruption and adulteration of God's Word from Genesis to Revelation (Proverbs 30:5-6).

Anti-biblical Word of Faith doctrines continue to gain open-arms acceptance among Pentecostals, Catholics, Charismatics, Messianic Jews, numerous congregations around the world, and Christian television. Anytime you look at the weekly forecast of different Christian networks, you will find men and women teaching false doctrines on faith, health, and wealth. Scriptural distortion is *engraved* in all false faith teachings.

The worldwide arena of false Word of Faith teachings includes The United States of America, Canada, Europe, Australia, Latin America, Great Britain, The Philippines, India, Asia, and Africa. Television and the Internet constantly promote and establish false faith teachings. Thus, millions have been exposed to the many false doctrines that will be presented and refuted throughout this book.

Those in charge of deciding what teachings and whom they allow on their Christian network are responsible to the LORD God for what they permit. If they allow false doctrines of sin about Jesus and His atonement, they are guilty of *blood deception* and the sins they permit from the mouths and the resources of false preachers.

Teaching false information about the Word of God is serious as the following verses verify: Proverbs 6:16-19; 30:5-6; John 8:44-47; Romans 16:17-18; Colossians 3:9-10; Revelation 21:7-8; 22:14-15. True believers who have been born-again of Jesus, the Lord of truth (John 14:6), are called to be God's ambassadors of truth for Christ (2 Corinthians 5:20).

Some of their false faith teachings will be shown to have an occult connection, and I don't know if they realize it. If those who claim to be Christians are using a teaching that is used in the occult, it does not prove they are demonic, but it does fall into what Paul wrote in 1 Timothy 4:1. Thus, it is possible that demon activity could be involved with manifesting false faith signs and wonders. Therefore, to close the door on the evil one, people must repent of all false doctrine when brought to their attention (2 Timothy 2:25-26).

If you are a parent, remember this; you are accountable for training and teaching your children in the way of the LORD (Proverbs 22:6). You train them for heaven if you teach them the truth about the real Jesus and *His* Gospel (Luke 24:45-47). If you teach them about a counterfeit gospel and "another Jesus" (2 Corinthians 11:3-4), causing them to stumble and misleading them, as do the many misled cults, the Lord Jesus said this sin would be costly (Matthew 18:6).

The way false teachers deceive people is by teaching Scripture in a way that the God-inspired writer (2 Timothy 3:16-17) did not record it to be taught. Sometimes they will proclaim, "The LORD told me this is what the verse means." But they distort verses by ignoring the full context of the verse, and the content of the verses before and after. Using "verse isolation" for establishing a doctrinal belief, while disregarding what the Bible says in other areas of Scripture about the topic, is the road to spiritual corruption. This leads to a dungeon of doctrinal deception.

In Isaiah 52:14, the prophet described how Israel's Messiah would be "marred more than any man, and His form more than the sons of men." By the time you finish reading this book, you will see that various false Word-Faith doctrines *have marred* the true spiritual identity and character of the real Jesus. Most definitely, the Jesus of the Worldwide Faith Movement is "another Jesus," *not* the Jesus Who came from heaven.

"By false faith," some have visualized and verbally created an unbiblical Jesus in place of the real Jesus for personal gain, as will be documented. The identity of God's *only* Messiah, Jesus of Nazareth, is critical when teaching about the LORD'S salvation. Defamation of Christ's nature, character, and His blood adds up to serious sin (2 Corinthians 5:10).

Danny Frigulti – April, 2017

Warning!

False doctrine is "Satan's dungeon of captivity."

Note: Though a Bible verse may not capitalize certain words, I have chosen to capitalize words such as "He," "Him," "His," "One," "Who," or any word referring to the Father, Son, or Holy Spirit.

Chapter 1

Laying a Foundation for Discernment

In this chapter, we will learn how to find the true context of verses in order to understand what the Bible teaches about a specific verse or topic. This type of learning produces discernment (a proper scrutiny or judgment), the ability to see the difference between truth and error. When careful discernment is used, it is harder to be deceived by false doctrine preachers.

Word of Faith ministers preach the truth sometimes, but they also mix truth with error in some of their teachings, and this leads people astray. Our Scriptural focus will be on exposing false teachings so that people will repent and not live constantly in the sin of false doctrine. More Christians need to remember that the sin of false doctrine leaves the door open for demonic influence (1 Timothy 4:1).

When studying a specific word or doing a topical study, pray often, and look at all the verses in a concordance where the word is used to reach an accurate understanding of the word or topic. Also, look at the verses before and after the verse you are seeking to know. Such dedicated study will draw you closer to the LORD, and give you His insight for your growth and steadfast truth in Christ.

False teachers isolate a verse or part of a verse, construct a new meaning (some call it a revelation from God), and then false doctrine is generated. They ignore the content before and after the verse they are corrupting.

Proper Scriptural understanding (honoring His Word) leads to correct teaching and glorifies the LORD (Psalm 119:11; 138:2). Choosing improper Scriptural understanding charts a dark path to deceptive teaching, establishes false doctrine, honors Satan (John 8:44), and lays a foundation for heresy. I will present some common verses false faith preachers distort with *their* own translation, and the correct God-inspired meaning will be shown.

Romans 4:17

The last part of this verse mentions that God "calls those things which are not (in existence) as though they were." Hyper-faith Christians are convinced this verse entitles them to speak miracles, prophecies, healings, and financial prosperity into existence just like God speaks, and the supernatural will happen. This verse does not teach that Christians can do miracles just like the LORD God!

Read verses 13-21 and the content will reveal these Scriptures are about Abraham, *not* for future miracles and healings through New Covenant followers of Messiah Jesus. The verse 17 context is focused on God saying what He did through Abraham and Sarah for the future.

In his book titled *The Power of I AM—Two Words That Will Change Your Life Today*, Joel Osteen writes:

> Romans 4 says to "call the things that are not as though they were." That simply means that you shouldn't talk about the way you are. Talk about the way you want to be.[1]

Joel Osteen's Romans 4 instruction is thoroughly out of context. He is teaching people to act like God and call into existence what they desire by using verse 17. Joel needs to teach more on prayer and submission to God's will (Hebrews 5:7; 1 John 5:14).

Charles Capps and his daughter Annette Capps teach you can use Romans 4:17 for buying property. This quote will provide a clear picture of what Word-Faith advocates believe about their faith, which causes the supernatural to transpire:

> I call those things that be not as though they were. I now call the property that fits my needs and desires and will be a blessing to me. I CALL YOU TO ME NOW IN JESUS'

6

NAME! I declare that God's highest and best is done in this matter and the angels are now working on my behalf. (Rom. 4:17).[2]

This misuse of God's Scripture ignores prayer (Philippians 4:6), His will (1 John 5:14), and has one acting as God.

2 Corinthians 5:7

This Scripture reads, "For we walk by faith, not by sight." The unstable/untaught (2 Peter 3:16) use this verse to teach that when you are sick, you *deny* you are sick, no matter what your health condition reveals. Then your faith will bring healing to your body, because Jesus died on the cross two thousand years ago to forgive you *and* heal your diseases. This false healing teaching will be refuted later in another chapter.

Read verses 1-6. Sickness or denying sickness are not mentioned leading up to verse 7. Verse 6 teaches when we are at home in the body, we are absent from the Lord. Verse 8 talks about preferring "to be absent from the body, and to be present with the Lord."

When people isolate a verse, such as verse 7, and decide to use it for teaching followers to "claim their healing by faith," they are rejecting clear Scriptural guidelines for understanding and accepting the context of God's inspired Word (2 Timothy 3:16). In all the healings Jesus and His disciples did, the sick were never taught to deny/ignore their physical malady or claim their healing "By faith" *before* it transpired. Christians who are sick don't live in denial. They seek the LORD and call upon the elders for prayer (James 5:14-18), or ask God to bestow a gift of healing for them.

Scripture confirms that dedicated servants of God were sick and Paul, who was given an apostolic healing ministry (2 Corinthians 12:12), did *not* tell them to ignore their problem (deny all physical symptoms and evidence), and claim their healing (Philippians 2:25-

29; 1 Timothy 5:23; 2 Timothy 4:20). These disciples of love and truth persevered through their ailments, and God did not grant them a gift of instant healing. People who instruct the sick to ignore their physical problem are not teaching healing in line with the Bible.

Philippians 2:9-10

Word of Faith teachers believe that since Philippians 2:9-10 states Jesus has the Name above all names, "By faith," they can use His Name to rebuke all sickness and disease. Here is their incorrect reasoning: Cancer and every disease have a name. Therefore, all diseases must bow the knee to the Name of Jesus when rebuked and be gone! These verses don't mention using Christ's Name to cure and heal the sick. However, Joyce Meyer chooses to disregard Scripture context by omitting verse 11, and teaches what Paul doesn't teach:

> Have you ever noticed that everything in this world has a name? Trees, people, bugs, buildings, streets, all our foods and all diseases have names. The name is Jesus is **above** every other name, and it contains so much more power than everything else in existence that every knee must bow to it and submit to its authority in all three realms—heaven, earth and under the earth.[3]

Paul clearly teaches in verses 10-11 that at the Name of Jesus every knee should bow in heaven, on earth, and under the earth, and every tongue confess that Jesus Christ is Lord to the glory of the Father. Have you heard of any scientific findings confirming cancer and all diseases have knees for bowing, and tongues for confessing Jesus is Lord?

These verses refer to a future time when God will judge the world through Jesus (2 Corinthians 5:10; Revelation 20:11-15). Because of Christ's sacrificial death of forgiveness on the cross and His physical resurrection from the dead (Romans 1:4; 1 Corinthians 15:1-8), He will judge all living beings. Therefore, all living beings in heaven (angels and forgiven people), on the earth (people still here and future people), and under the earth (all demons/evil spirits and all non-repentant souls left in Hades) will bow to Him eventually, and confess Jesus is Lord! (Revelation 20:11-15).

1 Chronicles 16:22

This verse reads, "Touch not mine anointed, and do my prophets no harm." Word of Faith ministers have used it for many years to silence the opponents of false faith doctrines. They say, "If you speak against the teachings of an anointed faith preaching minister, you will answer to God!" This verse is not about judging false doctrine. It's telling the people not to *physically* harm a prophet or a person whom God has anointed for an office of duty.

Chapter 17 of 1 Samuel records David's heroic effort to defeat Goliath. King Saul became jealous of David's ongoing success (chapters 18-19), sought to kill David (verse 19:1), and David fled for his life. David was pursued, but avoided being caught and killed.

In 1 Samuel 24:5, David cut off part of King Saul's skirt as he slept (verses 3-5). In verses 6 and 10, David explains that he is not to touch (physically harm) the LORD'S anointed, and again says the same in 26:9.

Though the context of not doing *physical harm* to King Saul is obvious and repeated, Jerry Savelle says, "The sword is symbolic of our words. You and I need to stop touching God's anointed with our words"[4] Savelle assumes David used a sword, rather than a knife to cut material from King Saul's skirt, but the word for sword is not mentioned in these "cutting" verses. A sword would be big and noisy for cutting Saul's skirt. But a knife, which was commonly carried for cutting meat, would make less noise to awaken Saul and display common sense. Furthermore, this setting does not say that the sword was "symbolic" of anything.

Are Word of Faith Televangelists Misleading Millions?

This is a classic example of how false faith teachers corrupt the Word of God. The clear and obvious context of physical harm is ignored. To protect their false teachings, they try to scare and silence people from obeying Scripture by testing all things (1 Thessalonians 5:21), and behaving like noble Bereans (Acts 17:11).

On page 7 of his book, *Touch Not God's Anointed,* Jerry Savelle says, "I know in my spirit that what you are about to read is a message straight from the Lord."[5] Look back at what he calls "a message straight from the Lord" in reference to the proper context of 1 Chronicles 16:22 when discussing "Touch not the Lord's anointed." His message doesn't line up with Scripture. Christians need to be careful about saying "The LORD told me," or any such rhetoric. A born-again person is *not* perfect or totally renewed in his spirit (2 Corinthians 4:16). Spiritual cleansing is needed (2 Corinthians 7:1).

It is Scriptural to "righteously" judge teachers and examine their verbal and written doctrinal presentations (John 7:24; Acts 17:11). Spirit-filled Christians abhor what is evil (false doctrine is evil) and cling to that which is good (Romans 12:9). We are called to "Prove all things; hold fast that which is good" (1 Thessalonians 5:21).

In reference to God's Word, the late Charles Capps wrote two bold statements that deserve our attention:

> If it doesn't agree with the *WORD*, you know *who* said that. The devil said it. *Don't you quote it.* If you do, that's his deception.[6]

Keep this quote in mind, because numerous Word-Faith teachings will be shown to *not* be in agreement with God's Word from chapter to chapter. He also said:

> To despise, reject, or even disagree with the Word opens the door to Satan. *If you despise the Word, you have invited destruction.*[7]

10

Charles Capps was a strong, outspoken Word of Faith and "confession of the Word" believer for decades prior to his passing away. If these two quotes are true, then the false doctrines in the Faith Movement have opened the door for Satan's doctrines of demons.

This chapter gave different examples of how to discern verses and understand the context. You have been given sufficient illustrations of how false teachers/authors misrepresent God's Word. With what was provided, you should be able to perceive the truth in the dozens of false doctrines to be unveiled in this book. Grasping the true meaning of Scripture honors His Word and glorifies the LORD (Psalm 138:2).

The next chapter will emphasize the importance of sound doctrine according to God's Word. In John 17:17, the Lord Jesus prayed that His followers would be *sanctified in truth,* and God's Word is truth. This prayer is Christ's fervent desire for those who will believe God's Word. They are to teach it accurately, proving they love Him (John 14:21-24). Those who are born-again (John 3:3-8; 1 Peter 1:23) are to bear Holy Spirit fruit (John 15:5) in all areas of their representation of Jesus. This fruit includes the sound doctrine they believe and teach.

Endnotes:
1. Joel Osteen, *The Power of I AM—Two Words That Will Change Your Life Today* (New York, New York: FaithWords, 2015), p. 8.
2. Charles & Annette Capps, *God's Creative Power For Finances* (England, Arkansas: Capps Publishing, 2004), pp. 33-34.
3. Joyce Meyer, *Be Healed in Jesus' Name* (New York, New York: Warner Faith Printing, 2002), pp. 58-59.
4. Jerry Savelle, *Touch Not God's Anointed The Danger of Judging Other Ministries* (Crowley, Texas: Jerry Savelle Ministies International, 2012), p. 23.
5. Ibid., p. 7.
6. Charles Capps, *The* Tongue—*A Creative Force* (England, Arkansas: Capps Publishing, 1995), p. 89.
7. Ibid., p. 120.

They also that erred in spirit shall come to understanding, and they that murmured shall learn doctrine (Isaiah 29:24).

And they continued steadfastly in the apostles' doctrine and fellowship, and in breaking of bread, and prayers (Acts 2:42).

Whoever transgresseth, and abideth not in the doctrine of Christ, hath not God. He that abideth in the doctrine of Christ, he hath both the Father and the Son (2 John 9).

The testimony of "the real Jesus" is the Spirit of prophecy (Revelation 19:10). The testimony of "another Jesus" is the spirit of *false* prophecy.

Chapter 2

The Importance of Sound Doctrine

Evil teachings are commonly taught daily by many faith teachers around the world. All false doctrine has the root and growing branches of improper interpretation of Scripture which leads to ongoing sin. Therefore, its fruit gives spiritual sickness to any who hear it and receive it in their spirit. Many who preach false faith doctrines look healthy on the outside, but because of their sin they are not healthy (spiritually clean) before the LORD.

True Christian doctrine originates from the proper interpretation of Scripture and bears good fruit (John 15:1-8). Paul recorded the importance/necessity of sound (true) doctrine in the following verses: 1 Timothy 1:3; 4:1, 6, 13, 16; 6:3; 2 Timothy 4:1-4; Titus 1:9. These verses verify that the LORD is very concerned about all doctrines and for good reason. If Christians allow false teachings to infiltrate Christianity, then the unity of the faith will be severed and division will blossom (Romans 16:17). Also, false doctrine allows demonic spirits (1 Timothy 4:1) evil freedom to deceive and counterfeit the works/presence of the Holy Spirit within the Body of Christ. This evil freedom is *increasing* among those involved with false faith doctrines.

As Paul prepared to leave Ephesus after extensive teaching for three years, he warned the Christians that when he was gone the following would occur:

> For I know this, that after my departing shall grievous wolves enter in among you, not sparing the flock. Also of your own selves shall men arise, speaking perverse things, to draw away disciples after them. Therefore watch, and remember, that by the space of three years I ceased not to warn every one night and day with tears (Acts 20:29-31).

Are Word of Faith Televangelists Misleading Millions?

The Holy Spirit warns Christians in the first century and in the future that among them will arise those who will speak perverse things, and pull away disciples after themselves. Counterfeit teachers enter with the sin of false doctrine in *their* heart to be used with evil intent. Paul labels these perverse word speakers as "grievous wolves," not fellow Christians. These wolves will attack the sheep with words of distortion to deceive them into leaving the flock of obedience. The Greek word for "perverse" in verse 30 is *diastrephō* which means:

to distort, twist … 'turned aside,' 'corrupted,' Acts 20:30.[1]

This definition is a false doctrine "blueprint" and accurate label for the false faith preachers. In order to draw those away who were taught about the real Jesus, a deceptive way would be to tell them they were not taught "all" God has provided for them in Christ's atonement. Then a distorted gospel like the one currently taught by false faith teachers could draw them away to place *their* faith in a false Jesus, and a so-called guaranteed healing and prosperity gospel. This is exactly what is occurring in various segments of "false faith Christianity" around the world.

False faith teachings can sound good, especially to those who are not grounded in Scripture, or are new converts. Acts 20:30 is a good prophetic description of the false Worldwide Faith Movement and its foundation which stretches back more than 50 years. Much of American Christianity has become comfort, materialism, and money. So the appeal of the "Health and Wealth gospel" fits right into the hearts and desires of many ignorant and greedy people.

The mind, when entertaining something with appealing benefits, has tremendous potential to deceive itself when it is fed by persuasive faith talkers who display an abundance of wealth to back their talk. The popular faith healing and prosperity preachers are viewed by their followers as "the anointed of God," thus making it hard for their loyal devotees to accept them as ever teaching anything contrary to the Word of God. Some of the people are in such awe of these faith teachers that "idolatry" is the perfect label for *their* focus on man, whereas the focus should always be on the Lord Jesus (Colossians 1:17-20).

It is time for "those who claim to be Christians" to stop being tossed around by every wind of doctrine proceeding from people talented with cunning craftiness, who lie in wait to deceive any who will listen to and accept their false teachings (Ephesians 4:14). We are commanded to test everything we hear, and hold fast *only* to what is good (1 Thessalonians 5:21).

A little leaven can raise a lump of problems (Galatians 5:7, 9). There is a huge amount of leaven in the many false doctrines promoted by false faith teachers. Their leaven of false doctrine needs to be removed, because it is spiritually infecting the Body of Christ. Their leaven of false teaching presents "another Jesus" and "a false atonement." This amounts to "another gospel" (2 Corinthians 11:3-4), a gospel that does not glorify God (Galatians 1:8-9).

Scriptural Guidelines for Sound Doctrine

As Christianity grew after Pentecost, Christian leaders were careful to establish only doctrine that was Scriptural (Acts 2:42). Never were isolated passages or parts of passages used to establish new doctrines, as has happened often in the false Faith Movement teachings. The apostles had knowledge of Old Covenant Scripture and also learned New Covenant teachings directly from Jesus. Using these two Sources, proper guidelines for sound doctrine became the established norm in Christianity.

Paul told Timothy to instruct certain men not to teach strange (false) doctrines (1 Timothy 1:3), as well as any other thing contrary to sound doctrine (verse 10). Also, Paul told Timothy to be nourished on the words of the faith and on the sound doctrine which he had been following (1 Timothy 4:6), and he was to pay close attention to his own teaching (verse 16). Constant "study and application" of God's Word reduces our chance of being snared by false doctrine or any evil, and is vital for proper spiritual growth (2 Timothy 2:15).

The verses in the previous paragraph teach the importance of paying close attention to our teachings and being nourished on true and sound doctrine. The Word-Faith Movement has a maze of different doctrines that will be shown to be unscriptural. Their teachings do not agree with the sound words of our Lord Jesus Christ (1 Timothy 6:3-5), because they teach "another Jesus" and a "different gospel" (2 Corinthians 11:3-4).

Christ's sound doctrine was guaranteed forgiveness of all sins and salvation for all who called upon Him (Matthew 26:28; Luke 19:10; 24:47), not guaranteed healing and financial gain for all. Therefore, we are charged in the presence of God and Christ to preach the Word, reprove and rebuke, for the time will come (that time is now) when they will not endure sound doctrine, but will desire to have their ears tickled and will follow after teachers in accordance with *their* own desires (2 Timothy 4:1-4). They will turn away from the truth about the real Jesus, as those who embrace false faith teachings *have done*, and worship and serve "another Jesus."

Verses 3 and 4 paint a sad, but true picture of the multitudes caught up in the arena of false faith doctrine ruling their lives. Of *their* own free will, they reject sound (true) doctrine and *choose* what they want to hear to satisfy *their* desires (verse 3).

False doctrines are devastating to the unity of the faith as verified in 2 Timothy 2:16-19. Hymenaeus and Philetus taught the resurrection had already occurred. This overthrew (upset) the faith of Christians. Assuredly, false faith teachings guaranteeing health and wealth have destroyed what *was* the true faith of some, and disillusioned others to the point that they no longer show zeal for a strong and personal relationship with the real Jesus. I have personally seen false Word of

Faith doctrines destroy a marriage, cause division in a very edifying and dynamic Bible study, and separate close friends.

Satan Snares Through False Doctrine

Paul writes in 2 Timothy 2:24-25 that Timothy is to be patient and gentle as he corrects and instructs those who are in opposition to the truth, if perhaps God will give them repentance which leads to acknowledging the truth. Deceived people (those involved with false doctrine) need God's help so "they may recover themselves out of the snare of the devil, who are taken captive by him at his will" (verse 26). The devil desires to snare Christians for the purpose of doing his will. Satan's will for us is to be involved in any area of sin, and the many false faith doctrines taught daily around the world are enslaving multitudes in sin.

The word "recover" in verse 26 will help us to understand why it is hard for people who follow false doctrine to acknowledge the truth when it is presented. The Greek word for "recover" is *ananēphō* which means:

> to return to soberness, as from a state of delirium or drunkenness ... is used in 2 Timothy 2:26, "may recover themselves," "return to soberness," said of those who, opposing the truth through accepting perversions of it, fall into the snare of the Devil, becoming intoxicated with error; for these recovery is possible only by "repentance unto the knowledge of truth." [2]

This definition is enlightening, for this Greek word is very expressive. Deceived people who teach and follow false doctrine do not function with a spiritually sober mind. Deception takes root when it is received and believed into practice. They are in opposition to the truth of God's Word because they "accept perversions" of the truth; they are "intoxicated with error." The only way they can escape the snare of doing the devil's will is to acknowledge the truth. Doctrinally deceived people need to pray for God to have mercy on them, and grant them "complete repentance" for their sinful false teachings about Jesus and any part of the Bible (verse 25).

Go back and read the definition of *ananēphō* again. This is a clear and straight-forward description of what can happen to Christians or anyone in another religion who follows the satanic father of lies (John 8:44) by believing his false doctrines. Numerous false teachings have spawned out of faith teaching churches for at least 50 years. The devil and his legions of demons have been given easy, wicked freedom to move to and fro in the Body of Christ deceiving multitudes around the world. When demons become aware of *any* ongoing false teachings in churches, in multimedia presentations, or in Bible studies, they know people are being taught doctrines of sin. This weakens the shield of faith (Ephesians 6:16).

This definition of spiritually/mentally impaired people who accept false doctrine is in line with drunks and addicted people who frequent parties or bars. Most of the time they think all is going well and they are in control, failing to accept and realize their intake of alcohol or drugs is controlling them. They drink their favorite drink or take their favorite drug to feel better, and find people who want to hear their stories and believe like they believe. Then they have more fellowship with deception, sin, and perhaps demon activity.

Often people who are snared by their focus on false faith doctrines try to find those who believe like them. They talk about what they have obtained and achieved through "their word of faith," "creative visualization," and "positive confession." I have witnessed this behavior on Christian television when "health and wealth" faith messages are broadcast. False doctrine produces false spirituality because of spiritual intoxication.

Consider this for understanding the power of doctrinal lies; those snared by false doctrine get up every day and *reinforce* their deception by confessing their false doctrine as truth, listening to someone teach falsely, reading false doctrine literature, or reading and quoting the Bible in a distorted and unstable manner that leads to spiritual destruction (2 Peter 3:16). This consistent reinforcement of doctrinal error *blocks* their mind from becoming spiritually sober. Their belief in false doctrine *opens* the door for constant deception, thus hindering the work of the Holy Spirit.

To show how stubborn, snared, and deceived some of these "faith and confession" people are, I will relate a phone conversation I had with a daughter whose father preached and authored some of the false Word of Faith doctrines that will be refuted in this book. Her father was deceased when I called her long distance. I explained that I had read a few of his books, found some doctrinal errors, and had written down some corrections. I asked her if I could send these to her so she could "consider making corrections" when new book printings were released. Here was her response:

"I believe everything my dad wrote was inspired by God. I won't change anything."

She didn't even want to take time to look at the truth. Can you now see why it is hard to get those who are deceived and snared by false faith doctrine to repent? Some are convinced that "their faith literature" is inspired by God, just like God inspired His chosen people to record the Bible. They see *their* writings as equal with the Bible, so to change or remove some of their materials would be an insult to the LORD. However, they fail to see that their false teachings continually insult the LORD and are offensive to Him, as they choose to cling to the sin of false doctrine.

This is why we must pray that "God may grant them repentance" leading to the knowledge of the truth. False doctrine constantly deceives, snares, resists truth, and keeps a mind spiritually impaired with doctrinal mistakes. Sobriety comes *only* through acknowledging true doctrine and confessing the sins of false doctrine.

Sound doctrine was emphasized immediately to new converts in the early Church (Acts 2:42). It will always be God's will for His people to be spiritually sober (1 Peter 5:8) and be nourished on sound doctrine. We are very important to God; He invested His Son in our lives (John 3:16) and gave His Holy Spirit to dwell within us, that we would have sober minds to serve the real Jesus. A sound and honest mind works hard to honor God's Word by walking in truth (2 John 4; 3 John 4) and avoids deception. Be humble and careful. Satan can demand to sift us as wheat, as he did Peter in Luke 22:31.

Scripture warns us about false teachers and false prophets in 2 Peter 2:1. They "bring in damnable heresies, even denying the Lord that bought them, and bring upon themselves swift destruction." They are sensual, malign Scriptural truth, make merchandise of people, promote greed, and exploit people (verses 2-8). This paints a graphic spiritual portrait of the misled Worldwide Faith Movement, as will be revealed in every chapter in this book.

In verses 1-3, Peter warns Christians about false teachers and false prophets (doctrinal wolves) as did Paul in Acts 20:28-31. Revelation 22:15 puts spiritual dogs (those who distort, reject God's true Word), sorcerers, whoremongers (immoral persons), idolaters and everyone who loves and *practices lying* in the same category and place. That category is one of non-repentant sinners, and their place is *outside* the Holy City of God. The LORD hates lying (false doctrine) because it blocks truth and rejects truth. This can bring devastating consequences to one's life, and cause people to end up in the lake of fire (Revelation 14:10-11; 20:10-15; 21:8).

Look back at Genesis 3:1-6 where Satan deceived Eve with a lie. She sins and then her husband follows her in sin. Since that time humanity has suffered immensely, all because of the beginning of lies upon the earth. There is no biblical teaching of a little lie or a white lie (1 John 2:21). Teaching false doctrine is a big sin, as is all sin. It is one of the many sins that put Jesus on the cross to suffer a horrible crucifixion for all our sins, transgressions, and iniquities.

Don't treat any false doctrine lightly. Treat it with repentance and remove its effects by memorizing truth from the Scriptures. Then teach the truth. Throw out all promotional material you have on any false doctrine (Acts 19:18-20).

Dozens of false teachings will be constantly exposed and refuted. All false teachers are ambassadors of false doctrine. They are not hearing from the Lord Jesus. Their overflowing reservoir of false doctrine *proves* they don't understand Scriptures the way the LORD intended verses understood and taught. Continually, they "proclaim deception" and place themselves in opposition to God's Word.

Romans 16:17-18 describes those who cause divisions and offenses contrary to the doctrine which was taught. They "serve not our Lord Jesus Christ, but their own belly; and by good words and fair speeches deceive the hearts of the simple." Verse 18 describes the way false faith preachers have taught for over fifty years. They have a persistent appetite for excess money, luxury, and fame because of their "new teaching revelations," which oppose God's truth.

With years of cunning experience, they have learned how to distort and twist teachings by stitching together parts of verses that appeal to themselves first. Then they present them boldly with elements of truth to manipulate listeners into accepting erroneous teachings. This is an attack upon the hearts of the simple, innocent, and unsuspecting. Faith-talking "health and wealth" preachers talk about "ushering in the kingdom of God with signs and wonders around the world." But their numerous false doctrines that will be uncovered in this book indicate they could be "ushering in the false doctrine kingdom of Satan," and weakening the Body of Christ.

Pastors and elders, you are shepherds and overseers of God's forgiven sheep. It is *your responsibility* to protect them (1 Peter 5:1-

4). You must protect those under your authority by exposing all false doctrines. Teach them Scriptural truth about God-pleasing love, faith, and sound doctrine. May God's gracious blessings be with all who undertake this difficult, but much needed task throughout the world.

In 1 John 4:1, we are told to not believe every spirit, but test the spirits to see if they are of God, because *many* false prophets are in the world. The Bible is the way the LORD wants us to test the spirit of what a so-called prophet teaches or writes, or what any teacher proclaims as truth. True prophets teach truth about God's Word; false prophets teach lies about God's Word. In Matthew 24:24, Jesus puts false prophets *and* false Christs in the same category. Their "great signs and wonders" are for deception.

The Worldwide Faith Movement has those who claim to be prophets of God, supposedly "receiving direct revelation" from Him. But they teach false doctrines about Jesus, healing, money, and His blood, as will be shown in different chapters. Also, many preachers who embrace various false doctrines say repeatedly they are "anointed by the Lord" to teach. However, when compared to Scripture, *their* words of false teaching *prove* they are false prophets and false teachers with a false anointing.

The Holy Spirit *does not* anoint false teachers and false prophets to spread deception about Bible topics and Jesus. They need to take Matthew 7:13-23 very seriously, because Satan can counterfeit the anointing with signs, wonders, and miracles (Exodus 7:10-12; 8:5-7; Deuteronomy 13:1-4; Matthew 24:5, 24; 2 Thessalonians 2:7-12; Revelation 13:13-14). Do not let any false doctrine intoxicate you and snare you into a world of deception!

Endnotes:

1. W. E. Vine, *An Expository Dictionary of New Testament Words* (Old Tappan, New Jersey: Fleming H. Revell Company, 1966), Vol. III. Lo-Ser, p. 180.
2. Ibid., Vol. III. Lo-Ser, p. 262.

Chapter 3

Is All Sickness/Disease From Satan?

Word of Faith teachings promote the belief that *all* sickness and disease is from Satan and his demons. Therefore, God has not, and will not chastise His people with sickness. They also say that no Christian should be sick, and if sickness happens it is because of: 1) sin in your life, 2) weak faith, or 3) you are not walking in love. We will look at various Scriptures to see if demons are responsible for *all* sickness and disease, and check to see if the sick were ever told to deny they were sick in order to receive their healing.

Also, we will view Scripture to find the LORD'S role in any area of sickness. Then we will look at verses where servants of God were sick and see if sin, weak faith, or lack of love are mentioned as the cause of their ailment.

A verse Word of Faith teachers distort and use to convince themselves and their followers that *all* sickness comes from demons is part of Matthew 18:16 which reads "… that in the mouth of two or three witnesses every word may be established." Jesus is quoting from Deuteronomy 19:15. The obvious context is two witnesses who confirm testimony about sin, *not* testimony of sickness.

Frederick K. C. Price ignores what Lord Jesus teaches about trespass/sin in Matthew 18:16. He selects two passages where demons cause affliction (Acts 10:38; Luke 13:11-16) and says, "I am perfectly convinced, from these two scriptures, that sickness and disease is of Satan."[1] Acts 10:38 is to be understood as Jesus "doing good and healing all that were oppressed of the devil." This is *not* a verse that teaches all sickness and disease are from demonic spirits, because forthcoming Scriptures in this section will prove otherwise.

Another Acts 10:38 point to consider as to why Peter preaches that Jesus healed all who were oppressed of the devil is this; demon activity was common in the Roman Empire because they worshipped various gods. Demonic worship welcomes evil spirits around the worshippers, and certain evil spirits cause sickness and disease. Peter is not only preaching salvation in this message (verse 43). He is also declaring that those who receive Jesus will not have to live in fear of evil spirits afflicting them with ongoing sickness and disease. They can call upon the authority of Jesus for help and deliverance.

Other misled faith teachers who believe that all sickness is from Satan are:

> All sickness, no matter where it comes from; birth, inheritance, injury—is from the devil.[2] (Larry Huch).

> According to Scripture, every sickness is directly related with demon activity.[3] (Guillermo Maldonado).

> Every disease is of the Adversary.[4] (Gossett & Kenyon).

Though the Bible does cite instances where demons are shown to be the cause of different physical problems (Matthew 12:22; 17:14-21; Mark 5:1-16; Luke 4:40-41), it also reveals other Scriptural sources of sickness that are not from demons, as will be shown.

In Matthew 8:1-4, a leper comes to Jesus to be cleansed of the disease. Jesus does not rebuke or cast a demon out of the person. The Law teaching about leprosy in Leviticus 13-14 never teaches that all leprosy is caused by demons. Matthew also mentions the mother of Peter's wife was sick with a fever and Jesus "touched her hand, and the fever left her" (verses 14-15). This teaching says "the fever left her." A demon did not leave her. More Scriptural proof that some diseases are not demonic are Matthew 9:27-30, Mark 7:32-35, and 8:22-25.

The Old Covenant records examples of God *directly* using disease/sickness to chastise His people, if needed, as cited in Leviticus

26:15-25; Numbers 11:33-34; 12:1-15; Deuteronomy 28:15-29; 2 Kings 15:1-6, and 1 Chronicles 21:1-14. Even the New Covenant *confirms* that God uses sickness, and even death to punish Christians who choose to sin (Acts 5:1-11; 1 Corinthians 11:20-32; read verses 28-30). And because of sin, our corrupt/cursed creation is another source of sickness (Romans 8:20-22). Excessive sun exposure causes skin cancer. Air pollution causes respiratory ailments. Contaminated water and food cause various physical ailments, and sometimes death. Clearly, the Bible teaches that demons are *not* responsible for all sickness and disease.

Also, the teaching that sin, weak faith, or not walking in love are the reasons Christians get sick is unscriptural as verified in Philippians 2:25-30, 1 Timothy 5:23, and 2 Timothy 4:20. None of these false faith beliefs/teachings are found as causes of the ailment/sickness in these verses. And these sick Christians were never told to deny their sickness to receive healing. Ignoring obvious biblical evidence, Creflo Dollar writes "Have you noticed that every time God deals with sickness and disease, He deals with sin as well?"[5] Jesus never taught the sin of an individual *always* caused every disease (John 9:1-8).

Since we have learned from the Scriptures that all sickness is not from demons, we can expose how Word-Faith believers deceive the ignorant into believing they should never be sick. They remind the sick that "greater is He Who is in you, than he (the devil) who is in the world" (1 John 4:4). They continue by saying, "Since you have the Holy Spirit and I do to, we can unite in prayer and command the sickness to leave." If the sickness does not leave, a common response from the person *not* sick is, "Well I released my faith; you need to release your faith and your healing will manifest." Word-Faith healers are known for this type of ministry. Did Jesus teach healing this way?

This next section will reveal how false teachers attack and degrade one of God's greatest and steadfast role models found in the Bible.

Was Job Upright and Blameless or a Sinner?

In *The Book of Job*, God's servant goes through immense loss and suffering as detailed in chapters 1-2. Though God refers to Job's character as upright and perfect (verses 1:1, 8; 2:3) and not involved with any sin, Satan was given permission to afflict Job with agonizing pain, loss of possessions, and loss of loved ones. A careful reading of chapters 1-2 will show Satan *never* went to the LORD and accused Job of any specific sin which would give him an opportunity to afflict Job. However, Word of Faith preachers say Job lived in the "sin of fear" and this opened the door for demonic afflictions. The "sin of fear" is never mentioned by God or Satan as an opening for demonic assault in chapters 1-2. Despite no evidence for the "sin of fear" as Job's lifestyle, the following faith-emphasizing authors and preachers make these comments:

> Job 1:4, 5 gives us insight that Job often operated out of fear rather than faith.[6] (Joyce Meyer).

> If we go around all day thinking about our fears, playing them over and over again in our minds, they become a reality. That's what Job said: "The thing I feared came upon me" (Job 3:25).[7] (Joel Osteen).

> You see, Satan tried to get God to pull the hedge down ... Satan didn't even know that the hedge was down. Job had pulled the hedge down.... As long as Job walked in *faith*, the wall—the hedge—was up. But when he started walking in unbelief and doubt the hedge was pulled down. Job pulled it down![8] (Frederick K. C. Price).

There is no mention of Job operating in fear rather than faith in verses 4-5. The opposite is true. Job operated in faith, not fear, by worshipping God with prayer and burnt offerings for his sons. God never told Job his early morning offerings indicated he was operating/living with the "sin of fear" in his life. The fear mentioned in Job 3:25 is not the "sin of fear," and Job says this *after* the demonic attack has been authorized by God. It is a reverent and appropriate fear of God with respect, for He is the Almighty and does as He wills (Job 1:21; Psalm 115:3; Daniel 4:35).

Job 1:9 declares that even Satan was aware of Job's respectful fear of the LORD. Satan wanted to attack and destroy Job in several ways to prove he worshipped the LORD for material blessings rather than truly being devoted in love to God for Who He is, not for what He gives. And no verse says Job pulled down his hedge of protection by "walking in unbelief and doubt."

Chapter 42 has a clear teaching and powerful warning for all. God was very angry with Job's friends who had not spoken right of the LORD as Job had (verse 7). They had accused Job of sin, and said sin was the cause of his problems, as false faith ministers do. However, God didn't label Job with the "sin of fear." God called Job His servant four times in verses 7-8. The LORD told Job's friends to offer a burnt offering because of their folly (false assessment that Job's sin brought all of these various punishments). Job prayed for his *deceived* friends (verse 10), and his painful, patient endurance was rewarded with a better blessing in his later years (verses 8-17).

In Ezekiel 14:14-20, the LORD mentions Noah, Daniel, and Job. The prophet does not say anything about Job being a person who was known for his "sin of fear." Rather, Ezekiel talks about "their righteousness" (all three of them). Jesus and His apostles never taught that Job lived in the "sin of fear" and was a bad example of faith.

Furthermore, James 5:11 says Job is remembered as an example of patience in the midst of suffering, not as an example of a man whose "sin of fear" dropped his hedge of protection and allowed Satan to destroy his property and family members (Job 1). Those who have taught falsely on Job's ordeal need to repent. They have dishonored Job and God's Scripture.

In his book, *The Spreading Flame*, author F. F. Bruce tells us, "When Alexandria was devastated by an outbreak of plague in the middle of the third century, Dionysius, bishop of the church in that city, describes the devotion with which Christians tended the sick, often catching the plague and dying of it themselves in consequence."[9] These Christians showed abundant love and faith in service to the sick, and it cost them their lives. They contracted the plague, were sick, and still glorified the LORD while caring for others till they died. Such love fulfills John 15:13, and will always be needed and appreciated.

Praying for the Sick—James 5

James 5:14-18 provides instruction on how to pray for the sick in the Body of Christ. The sick are to call for the elders. Admitting you are sick is not a negative confession as some teach, and does not show lack of faith. Jesus never taught that admitting you are sick showed a negative attitude or lack of faith when healing multitudes. It shows you have a need, and by faith in God you are coming to the elders for healing prayer. This prayer can be for spiritual or physical healing. The Greek word for healed in verse 16 is *iaomai* and can refer to spiritual inner healing (Matthew 13:15) and physical healing (Luke 6:18). This word is also used in Luke 4:18.

Elders should be men of prayer, know the Word to teach it as God intended (Acts 6:2-4), be able to refute false teachings, lead their household in the LORD'S way, live above reproach, and always be prepared to pray for the sick (1 Timothy 3:1-7; Titus 1:5-9). Becoming an elder does not mean a person automatically receives the gift(s) of healing that is mentioned in 1 Corinthians 12:9, 11. This gift is given by God's grace and His will. With this in mind, we can look at the prayer of faith and the oil for anointing.

Is All Sickness/Disease From Satan?

When the sick request prayer, counsel should be given to inquire if any sin needs to be confessed (verse 15). The application of oil does not guarantee a miraculous healing. Medicinally, oil and wine were used for healing wounds during the time of Christ, as recorded in the story of the Good Samaritan (Luke 10:34). Today, we have more creams, ointments, and antibiotics.

The Greek word for anoint in verse 14 is not *chirō* which is used in sacred and symbolical anointings (Christ, the anointed of God, Luke 4:18; Acts 4:27; 10:38; Hebrews 1:9). The word for anoint is *aleiphō* and is a general term used for anointing of any kind (Matthew 6:17; Mark 16:1; Luke 7:38, 46; James 5:14).[10]

Oiling with oil (commonly placed on the forehead now days) can bring comfort and relaxation to the one seeking healing. But the power is *not* in the oil; it's in the prayer of faith. Notice that the prayer of faith is the responsibility of the elders, not the one seeking healing. The faith one needs when seeking healing is repentance and asking for prayer. Should physical healing not transpire, we are not to blame the sick person.

Therefore, if a sick person desires healing, the elders must spend time in prayer to see if it is God's will to bring healing to the sick person. Only *after* discerning it is God's will to heal the sick person can the elders pray "the prayer of faith." Otherwise, their prayer is more of a prayer of spiritual comfort. Elijah is mentioned as the example for the elders concerning the prayer of faith (verses 17-18 and 1 Kings, chapters 17-18).

Sometimes it may require fasting to discern God's healing will, and He may also require that the elders fast and pray more than once for the same person. This is an area of *constant responsibility* to the LORD where elders are to be active in their faith to minister to the needs of those who come for any type of healing or counsel. Pastors, are the elders in your congregation biblically qualified to serve?

Concerning disease, there is another James 5:14-18 teaching we need to honor. If all sickness is from demons as some falsely teach, then this would be the place to teach it. Then the elders could pray and rebuke the demonic illness in the Name (authority) of Jesus. But the Scripture, in leading the elders to pray for the sick, does not say to view all sickness as a demonic affliction.

Endnotes:

1. Frederick K. C. Price, *Is Healing for All?* (Los Angeles, California: Faith One Publishing, 2015), p. 7.
2. Larry Huch, *The 7 Places Jesus Shed His Blood* (New Kensington, Pennsylvania: Whitaker House, 2004), p. 41.
3. Guillermo Maldonado, *Jesus Heals Your Sickness Today!* (Miami, Florida: ERJ Publications, 2009), p. 23.
4. Don Gossett & E. W. Kenyon, *The Power of Your Words* (New Kensington, Pennsylvania: Whitaker House, 1981), p. 63.
5. Creflo A. Dollar Jr., *How To Obtain Healing* (College Park, GA: Creflo Dollar Ministries, 1999), p. 16.
6. Joyce Meyer, *Be Healed In Jesus' Name* (Fenton, Missouri: Warner Books, 2002), p. 43.
7. Joel Osteen, *I Declare 31 Promises to Speak Over Your Life* (New York, New York: FaithWords, 2013), p. 135.
8. Frederick K. C. Price, *Is Healing for All?* (Los Angeles, California: Faith One Publishing, 2015), pp. 9, 10.
9. F. F. Bruce, *The Spreading Flame* (Grand Rapids, Michigan: Wm. B. Eerdmans Publishing Company, 1979), p. 191.
10. W. E. Vine, *An Expository Dictionary of New Testament Words* (Old Tappan, New Jersey: Fleming H. Revell, 1966), p. 58.

Chapter 4

Creative Visualization: Are Christians gods?

For decades, Word-Faith people have taught "creative visualization" to enhance a Christian's prayer life. This process of visualization encourages a person to create a picture or image (also called mental imagery) in their mind as if it has already happened as they desire, and then seek the help of supernatural power to make their created vision manifest/happen. This is combined with "positive confession" to activate the supernatural spiritual realm. When done, these two components of visual and verbal effort have the spiritual potential to connect users to the wrong spiritual realm, a realm where demons are found.

Normal visualization imagines pictures of events in our mind that have occurred or might happen (daydreaming). Athletes picture or imagine, with concentrated focus, the free throw going into the basket or picture the body movement needed to perform in a specific event. These examples of everyday visualization do not require the mind to engage in supernatural powers to aid them in becoming a reality.

Dr. David Yonggi Cho, a Korean pastor, teaches that "Through visualizing and dreaming you can incubate your future and hatch the results."[1] Charles Capps (1934-2014) taught, "The best way to get the image in you of the thing hoped for, is with *your own words*."[2] (italics in original). Jerry Savelle says:

> If you need money, start creating an image of yourself with money by meditating God's Word.... Meditate on verses like this one: (Philippians 4:19). God will paint a picture on the canvas of your heart of your needs being met. That image will be more real than what your physical eyes see.[3]

Are Word of Faith Televangelists Misleading Millions?

When teaching on prayer, Jesus *never* used or taught His disciples "imaging," "dreaming," "vision-casting," or "visualizing" personal desires for money or healing (Matthew 6:9-13; John 14:13-14). Our prayer Teacher "offered up prayers and supplications" (Hebrews 5:7).

Creative visualization is actually an occult activity being used by many Christians around the world. Those claiming to be followers of the Lord Jesus must renounce this occult activity, because it is used in magick according to the following references:

> What is the purpose of creative visualization? To make real what is not yet real. **If you can make it real in your mind/body, then it will manifest in the world.** So creative visualization is a key component to making magick.[4]

> CREATIVE VISUALIZATION is the name for a Magical-Occult-Operation.[5]

Evil abides in "creative visualization" as this final information will confirm:

> This is a very simple visualization technique.... Imagine that there is a long cord attached to the base of your spine, extending down through the floor and way down into the earth. If you wish, you can imagine that this is like the root of a tree, growing deep into the ground. This is called a "grounding cord." Now imagine that the energy of the earth is flowing up through this cord (and up through the soles of your feet if you are sitting in a chair) and flowing up through all parts of your body, and out through the top of your head. Picture this until you really feel the flow well established. Now imagine that the energy of the cosmos is flowing in through the top of your head, through your body, and down through your grounding cord and your feet into the earth.[6]

Creative Visualization: Are Christians gods?

Insight: This explicit visualization teaching directs the participant to imagine (visualize) a grounding cord "way down into the earth" to get a power flow. If there is a power flow "way down into the earth" then what is the source of this power flow? According to the Bible, this power flow is demon activity. The Bible teaches that demons are aware of a place called the "abyss" or "the deep" (Luke 8:30-31), a region found in the depths of the earth. This area or deep earth realm is mentioned in Revelation 11:7 where it talks about "the beast that ascends or comes up out of the bottomless pit" and kills people. Revelation 17:8 says the beast "shall ascend out of the bottomless pit." Also, Revelation 20:1-3 records good news that an angel, who has the key to the bottomless pit, will bind up the dragon, that old serpent, which is the Devil (Satan), and *cast him down* into the bottomless pit for a thousand years. The location of this bottomless pit is not in outer space, but "way down into the earth." So the power coming to those who are involved with "creative visualization," or use a "grounding cord" to tap into power "way down into the earth" is not from the Lord Jesus. It is from demons that dwell in the depths and various regions of the lower earth. For more study on the pit of hell (*sheol* in Hebrew) and where it is found, look at Isaiah 14:15 "brought down to hell," Ezekiel 26:20 "descend into the pit," "in the low parts of the earth," "that go down to the pit," and Ezekiel 31:16, "when I cast him down to hell with them that descend into the pit."

These sources reveal and confirm the occult/demonic nature of "creative visualization." "Prayer picturing" (creative visualization) is not biblical prayer. It's occult prayer. Christians are to pray/ask in Jesus' Name (John 14:13) and in accordance with God's will (1 John 5:14-15), not in accordance with our pictured and visualized will. From Genesis to Revelation, there is not one teaching of God's people using "creative visualization" for any reason, because it is wrong.

Were Adam and Eve gods?

Some Word-Faith preachers believe man was "a god" in the beginning of creation, but lost the title when Adam and Eve sinned in the Garden of Eden. They teach Christians will become gods when they receive Jesus (John 1:12), confess Him as Lord (Romans 10:9-10), and are born-again (John 3:3-8).

Kenneth Copeland believes "Adam was created in God's class," and *"Man had total authority to rule as a god over every living creature on earth, and he was to rule by speaking words."*[7] However, Mr. Copeland does not list any Scriptures from Genesis 1-3 to support his quoted teachings, because there aren't any.

Quotes from Dr. Creflo Dollar's 2002 edition, *The Image Of Righteousness You're More Than You Know,*[8] will be listed to illustrate his belief and then compared to Scripture:

> When God made Adam, He made an exact duplicate of Himself (page 83).

> God in heaven had made Adam god of the earth. Adam was crowned god of all physical things formed from the dust of the earth: Let him have dominion (page 85).

> All of God's handiwork was now placed in the authority of the god of the earth—Adam.... God wanted a god on the earth like He was God in heaven (page 85).

> God was training a god in the earth (page 86).

> Adam had authority. He was god of this physical realm just as God was God of the spiritual realm. Adam was god of this planet and all the handiwork of God (page 86).

> Like Jesus, there is a price to pay once you declare that you share equality with God (page 89).

Creative Visualization: Are Christians gods?

None of these excerpts from Pastor Dollar's book are found in the Genesis account when God created man because: 1) It is impossible for God to make Adam "an exact duplicate of Himself." God has existed eternally; Adam had a beginning (Genesis 5:2). 2) No verse says God made Adam "god of the earth" and crowned him god of all physical things formed. 3) The Creator doesn't need "a god" on the earth like He is God in heaven. God can easily run and control all of His creation (Psalm 24:1). 4) The LORD does not train any man to be a god. 5) God is God of all He created, both physically and spiritually. 6) Though we are joint heirs with Jesus, we will never be equal with God. Jesus never said His followers would "share equality" with God when they were born-again.

Even the great foundation-laying apostles (Ephesians 4:11), who recorded Scripture, never claimed they were equal with God. Man had a beginning. Messiah Jesus has existed from eternity (Micah 5:2). He is the eternal Word Who created all things (John 1:1-3). What is created (man) can *never* be equal with the eternal Creator.

Exodus 7:1 is also a verse taught by Word-Faith ministers to excite new converts to believe they have become gods. Let's look at this verse and break it down:

> And the Lord said unto Moses, see I have made thee a god to Pharaoh: and Aaron thy brother shall be thy prophet.

Like us, Moses was only a man with a human nature. What God is communicating to Moses in Exodus 7:1 is this: "When I finish demonstrating My power to Pharaoh through you, he will see you as a god." Though Moses displayed supernatural power which made him appear to be "a god" to Pharaoh, he *never* claimed to be "a god" during or after the LORD used him to *plague* Pharaoh. The supernatural power came from God, not Moses.

In chapter 11 of Hebrews, Moses is *not* recorded and remembered as "a god," but as an example of faith (verses 23-29). Great faith does not make one "a god." It makes one a great servant of obedience who reveres the Almighty God. If becoming a follower of Messiah Jesus restores lost "godhood" to as many as believe, why didn't Peter preach this in his Pentecost message? Repenting and receiving Jesus of Nazareth as Lord and Savior guarantees the gift of the Holy Spirit and forgiveness (Acts 2:38), not becoming "a god."

Definitely, in *The Acts of the Apostles,* the opportunity was available to tell the listeners, if true, that New Covenant converts would become "gods" (Acts 14:6-18; 17:16-32). Yet in each of these examples where "gods" were part of the culture, Paul directs their attention away from the topic of being "a god," and moves their attention to the Gospel of forgiveness and love.

Psalm 82 and John 10:24-38

Still, some believe when Jesus quoted Psalm 82:6, while talking to the Jews in John 10:24-38, that this proves even Jesus knew and recognized these people were "gods." The Jews addressed in this setting were not devoted followers of Jesus, and certainly not born-again of the Holy Spirit, Who was to come "after" Christ's crucifixion and resurrection (John 14:26; 15:26; 16:7; Acts 1:4-8). So it's obvious they could not have been "gods." His use of Psalm 82:6 in reference to "gods" needs proper understanding to discern what Jesus meant.

In John 10:24, the Jews question Jesus wanting to know if He is the Christ (Messiah). He responds in verses 25-29 by mentioning the works He has done in His Father's Name, His sheep hear His voice, and follow Him to eternal life. In verse 30 He claims, "I and My Father are one." The Jews picked up stones to stone Him for blasphemy (verse 33), because they understood His use of the word "one" (*hen*) meant claiming equality with God, which was blasphemy. Then Jesus directs them to Scripture from Psalm 82:6 where God referred to the unjust judges of Israel hundreds of years earlier.

Creative Visualization: Are Christians gods?

The beginning of Psalm 82 shows the LORD is exposing His people responsible for injustice and accepting the wicked (verse 2). Such behavior was found in the heathen and pagan nations where rulers called themselves "gods." God had told them to defend the poor and fatherless, and deliver the afflicted and needy because they lacked understanding and walked in darkness (verses 3-5).

Verse 6 says, "I have said, Ye are gods; and all of you are children of the Most High." Then in verse 7 He tells them, "But ye shall die like men, and fall like one of the princes." This verse shows their mere mortality as men. They never should have viewed themselves "as gods" or *acted* like "gods" by abusing their power when judging the people on behalf of the LORD.

They no longer followed God's instructions. In place of the Holy guidelines they were given from the LORD, they had chosen their own path of evil judgment. They were already called children of the Most High, but this was not good enough for them. The LORD never appointed them "as gods." Yet they *acted* like "gods," so He referred to them "as gods" to show them how blatant their sins of injustice were and how repulsive their attitude had become.

If this Psalm is truly teaching it's acceptable to be "a god" then why would verse 1 say that "He *judges* among the gods?" The answer is clear. He is not rewarding them for their good behavior. These rulers in Israel had used their authority in an "I am a god" way (their way) instead of in God's compassionate way. Because of their rebellion against His laws and guidelines, He referred to them "as gods" of personal authority, rather than His merciful judges and rulers. He was telling them how evil they were as judges.

The Israelites knew from the teachings of Moses how wicked the nations and demonic pagan cultures were that believed in man as "a god" or believed in demonic gods (Exodus 12:12; Deuteronomy 6:14; 13:1-4). It was a rebuke and shameful to be called "a god," and be identified with the demon-worshipping nations and the demonic angels who had rebelled against God. This should serve as a strong warning to anyone who claims to be "a god."

Now that Psalm 82 has some clarification, we can move on to John 10:34-36 where Jesus says to those who are angry with Him:

> Is it not written in your law, I said, Ye are gods? If He called them gods, unto whom the Word of God came, and the Scripture cannot be broken; Say ye of Him, Whom the Father hath sanctified, and sent into the world, Thou blasphemes; because I said, I am the Son of God?

Their response was not "Thank you Jesus for recognizing we are gods," because they knew it was sin to be involved with any god but the true God of Israel.

When Jesus mentioned His Father and Himself in verse 30, He was talking about two separate persons. As He refers to Himself as "the Son of God" in verse 36 (this means He is of the same eternal spiritual nature as His heavenly Father), He then mentions the works of His Father through Him (verse 38). What Jesus is saying to the Jews in context at this setting is this: "Your rebellious forefathers acted like gods and did not follow the Law of God. They were rebuked in Psalm 82. Now, as leaders of Israel, you cannot discern Who is in your midst, because you will not accept My works and the Scriptures from the Law that identify Me as the Messiah. In Psalm 82 they were not stoned for blasphemy because they behaved like gods in judging the people improperly, so why do you seek to stone Me for My many good works proving I am the Son of God?"

An accurate understanding of Psalm 82, and how Jesus used it in John 10:34, verifies that in no way did Jesus teach followers of the true God to refer to themselves "as gods." Also, Jesus *never* taught when you receive the Holy Spirit at spiritual rebirth you are now "a god." If you still have trouble believing this, then look carefully at these sections of Scripture in *The Acts of the Apostles*: chapters 2:38-

41; 8:14-17; 10:34-48. When the apostles were preaching to potential converts to follow Jesus, they *never* taught that if you become a Christian you also become "a god."

Isaiah 61:6 calls God's people "priests of the LORD" and "ministers of God." The prophet Isaiah does not call the LORD'S people "gods." However, some modern day *false* faith prophets and misled faith teachers do. So whom will you believe; Isaiah, who was inspired by the Holy Spirit, or a faith teacher who *supposedly* hears directly from God? Also, 1 Peter 2:9 says we are a "royal priesthood," and Revelation 1:6 states that Jesus "hath made us kings and priests unto God and His Father." When we do reign, we reign as priests of our heavenly Father and Christ, not "as gods" of our heavenly Father and Christ (Revelation 20:6).

Does the Bible show exactly how this "You can be a god" doctrine originated? Yes it does. This evil, deceptive teaching of demonic rebellion is found in Genesis 3:1-5. The serpent (Satan) is in the Garden of Eden. He intends to convince Eve that is it acceptable to disobey God's instruction about staying away from a specific tree in the midst of the Garden. She continues to listen to Satan and he tells her "that in the day ye eat thereof, then your eyes shall be opened, and ye shall be *as gods*, knowing good and evil" (emphasis mine).

Satan deceives Eve into believing she will become "a god" because of knowledge of good and evil. What a lie! The LORD did not tell Adam and Eve they were "gods" *before* they sinned, and by obeying Satan's lie about knowing good and evil, they did not become "gods" *after* they sinned. Believing you can become "a god" is not a Holy Spirit teaching.

Anton LaVey, the founder of the infamous Church of Satan, stated: "Every man is a god if he chooses to recognize himself as one."[9] True servants of the Lord Jesus choose to recognize themselves as ambassadors for Christ (2 Corinthians 5:20), not "gods."

The LORD warns people in Genesis 3:1-5 that the satanic serpent will tempt humanity to believe they can become "gods." Yet multitudes have rejected this *obvious warning* throughout history. People in the Worldwide Faith Movement, who claim they are Christians, continue to ignore this warning about believing "You can be a god." They have a choice to make; they can follow and serve Jesus and not claim to be "gods." Or they can remain in sin, believing they "are gods." Is it time to pray and repent of your "I am a god" sin, or are you spiritually clean before Lord Jesus concerning this matter?

Endnotes:

1. Dr. David Yonggi Cho, *The Fourth Dimension Volume One* (Alachua, Florida: Bridge-Logos Publishers, 1979), p. 32.
2. Charles Capps, *Faith and Confession* (England, Arkansas: Capps Publishing, 1987) p. 22.
3. Jerry Savelle, *The Nature of Faith* (Crowley, Texas: Jerry Savelle Ministries, 2009), p. 42.
4. http://www.wicca-spirituality.com/creative-visualization.html
5. Ophiel, *The Art and Practice of Gettings Things Through Creative Visualization* (San Francisco, California: Peach Publishing Co., 1968), p. 1.
6. Shakti Gawain, *Creative Visualization* (Novato, California: Nataraj Publishing, 1995), pp. 89, 90.
7. Kenneth Copeland, *The Power Of The Tongue* (Fort Worth, Texas: Kenneth Copeland Publications, 1980), pp. 6, 7.
8. Dr. Creflo A. Dollar JR., *The Image of Righteousness You're More Than You Know* (Tulsa, Ok: Harrison House Inc., 2002), pp. 83, 85, 86, 89.
9. Anton Szandor LaVey, *The Satanic Bible* (New York, New York: Avon Books, 1969), p. 96. (This quote is from the book *Tongues, Prosperity, & Godhood* by Dr. Cathy Burns, 2001), p. 92.

Chapter 5

Is Positive Confession Pleasing to God?

A popular Word of Faith teaching is "positive confession," also called "confessing God's Word," "Word-confession," "name it (what you want from God) and claim it," "confession of the Word brings possession of what your faith believes," "speaking faith decrees and declarations," and "You can have what you say."[1] This opening sentence gives "positive confession" its definition. Obviously this doctrine has nothing to do with biblical prayer. It's all about finding verses you believe God has already ordained for you, or a specific need you believe you're entitled to claim. Then you "confess" your faith claim (verse selection) out loud.

Common "positive confessions" usually refer to physical healing and money, because Word-Faith people believe the shed blood, death, and resurrection of Jesus guarantees them forgiveness of sins, health, and wealth. This heretical atonement belief will be refuted later.

As you read through this chapter, keep in mind that there is no place in the Bible where the words "positive" and "confession" are found together when we are being taught about prayer or presenting our needs before the LORD. Yet, false faith teaching ministries are convincing many followers that "positive confession" is better than prayer. Some believe when your faith reaches a certain level, you "claim and confess" your desires or needs rather than devoting yourself to prayer (Romans 12:12; Colossians 4:2), or praying consistently (1 Thessalonians 5:17).

A careful look at how and where the word "confession" is used in Scripture will confirm the proper use of "confession." We will also inspect areas where the word "confession" was placed by the Holy Spirit to see if the word "positive" is ever found with it. Let's look at New Testament verses that use the words "confession" or "confess," and learn from their context. In some verses, the KJV uses the word "profession," but it does not change the context. The writer's intent is clear.

Matthew 10:32, Luke 12:8, John 9:22, 12:42, Romans 10:9, and Philippians 2:11 all mention confession about Jesus and His Lordship. James 5:16 and 1 John 1:9 cite confess your sins, and 2 John 7 is a heretic test for confessing whether or not Jesus has come fully in the flesh. Revelation 3:5 says Jesus will confess the names of overcomers before His Father and the angels. The Greek words for "confess" or "confession" in these verses are *homologeō* and *exomologeō*. They mean:

> to speak the same thing ... (a) to confess, declare, admit, John 1:20 ... and (a) of a public acknowledgment or confession of sins, Matt. 3:6.[2]

Though these two words indicate a strong conviction in what one believes, neither word is found in a New Testament verse teaching Christians to use "positive confession" for healing or money. Hebrews 3:1, 4:14, and 10:21-23 refer to a Christian's confession of Jesus as the Son of God, High Priest, or holding on to the faith. The word for "confession" in these Scriptures is a noun (*homologia*) and "denotes confession, by acknowledgement of the truth."[3] None of the verses listed teach "positive confession" for speaking forth healings, miracles, or prosperity.

Several "word confession" teachings from Word of Faith and healing preachers will be listed to verify what they believe. This will confirm how they have deceived themselves and many who are not grounded in the accurate contextual meaning of "confession."

Charles Capps: *The Tongue—A Creative Force*

Words are the most powerful thing in the universe.[4]

Truth: Jesus didn't teach this. Mr. Capps is wrong. From page 1 throughout his book, he places too much power in spoken words to set up the reader to believe "positive confession" is an acceptable Christian lifestyle. The LORD, without saying a word, is the most powerful in His created universe.

Capps: Then He spoke into my spirit some things that totally transformed my life. He said … *You are under an attack of the evil one* and I can't do anything about it. *You have bound Me by the words of your own mouth.* And it is not going to get any better until you change your confessions and begin to agree with My Word.[5] (italics in original).

Truth: No verse in the Bible says our words can bind the Almighty God from doing as He pleases (Psalm 115:3). Such a belief implies that man's words have authority over God's power and sovereign rule.

Charles Capps: *Faith and Confession*

Confession is to your faith as thrust is to an airplane.[6]

Truth: No verse teaches this belief.

Capps: Confession is saying what God says in His Word. *Confession is agreeing with God.*[7]

Truth: This is a true statement. However, some forthcoming information from Scripture will prove repeatedly that he is not presenting the Bible correctly on the meaning of "confession."

Capps: *Confession of God's Word works for you because it sets the law of faith in motion.*[8]

Truth: Mr. Capps presents this teaching without any biblical foundation. No verse teaches there is a "law of faith" that sets "confession of God's Word" in motion.

Capps: *Confessing God's Word works for you because it puts the angels to work for you.*[9]

Truth: Our words or confessions do not put angels to work for us. All angels are in subjection to the Lord (Psalm 103:20-21; 1 Peter 3:22). Jesus directs angelic work, not Christians. While on the earth, Jesus did not tell angels how to work for Him (Matthew 26:53).

Capps: Some say, "That's just positive thinking or mind over matter." No. *It's the principle of God and the power of His Word over all matter.* It's God's method. We are created in the image of God and we operate in His principles[10]

Truth: Though we are created in God's image (Genesis 1:26-27), the verses in Genesis 1-2 *never* teach we can operate in His principles of supernatural power by using "His word control" over all matter.

Dr. David Yonggi Cho: *The Fourth Dimension Volume One*

As well as you can release Jesus' power through your spoken word, you can also create the presence of Christ. If you do not speak the word of faith clearly, Christ can never be released.[11]

Truth: Our spoken words do not create the presence of Christ. He is always with us (Matthew 28:20), and is able to do beyond what we ask or speak (Ephesians 3:20-21).

Cho: Remember that Christ is depending on you and your spoken word to release His presence. What are you going to do with this Jesus who is riding on your tongue? Are you going to release Him for the blessing of others? Or are you going to lock Him up with a still tongue and a closed mouth?[12]

Truth: Jesus didn't teach He would ride on our tongue, and that we release Him or lock Him up with our will. The belief of some who claim to be Christians can at times be both sad and ridiculous, especially when they don't use Scriptural support.

Gloria Copeland: *God's Will is Prosperity*

Speak whatever you desire to come to pass in the name of Jesus. Take authority over the money you need and command it to come to you. Whatever you say will come to pass.[13]

Truth: This instruction is derived from Mark 11:23-24. People forget that Mark 11:23 is connected to verse 22. The withering of the fig tree is a miracle, not a daily happening. Miracles manifest according to God's will, *not* our spoken word of faith (1 Corinthians 12:10-11). As our Holy role model, Jesus never commanded money to be sent to Him or His disciples.

Creflo Dollar: *The Image of Righteousness*

One part of man that is like God is the creative part: the ability to speak and create. That is why our confessions are so important.[14]

Truth: No Scripture links confessions as "creative ability" to speak God's Word. Talking about the LORD'S Word in *proper context* will always be sufficient and glorify Him!

E. W. Kenyon & Don Gossett: *Speak Life*

Refuse to make a bad confession. Refuse to make a negative confession. Repudiate a dual confession where you are saying at one moment "By His stripes, I am healed" and at the next moment "But the pain is still there." Your negative confession denies the healing Scripture, and you will go on in defeat.[15]

Truth: The LORD heals as He wills (1 Corinthians 12:11). Nowhere in the New Covenant do we find the apostles telling people to confess "By His stripes I am healed," and that a negative confession denies healing.

T. L. Osborn: *Healing The Sick A Living Classic*

When you declare, **By his stripes, I am healed**, your words bind Satan's hands. He is defeated and he knows it.[16]

Truth: By His stripes you are healed is cited in Isaiah 53:5 and 1 Peter 2:24. Nothing within, before, or after these verses mentions binding Satan to receive healing. Healing is God's will, not ours (1 Corinthians 12:9, 11).

Osborn: The confessions of **I am the Lord who heals you** and **by his stripes, I am healed** always precede the manifestation of healing, just as the confession of Jesus Christ as Lord and savior always precedes the experience of salvation. (Rom. 10:9-10).[17]

Truth: The apostles never taught confession always precedes healing in any New Testament writing. Salvation and healing are two different issues. God's will is that all should come to repentance, not that all should be physically healed (2 Peter 3:9).

Osborn: Speak to your disease or sickness, calling it by name. Command it in Jesus' name to leave your body.[18]

Truth: Jesus didn't instruct His apostles to teach healing in this manner. Nor did Paul tell the sick disciples in Philippians 2:25-29, 1 Timothy 5:23, and 2 Timothy 4:20 to command their illness or sickness to leave in Jesus' Name, and Paul knew the truth about Holy Spirit healing power (2 Corinthians 12:12).

John Osteen: *There is a Miracle in Your Mouth*

If you want to change your life, you have to change your confession. The miracle is in your mouth.[19]

Truth: Miracles happen according to God's will, not man's mouth (1 Corinthians 12:10-11).

Rod Parsley: *Your Harvest is Come*

When God created man, He gave him the same creative ability He possessed to speak things into being because He formed man in His image.[20]

Truth: A careful reading of Genesis 1:26-27 doesn't mention anything about God giving mankind the same supernatural "creative ability to speak things into being" when He created humanity. The LORD spoke and created all things into being. Man was given dominion over what was already created, not the power to continue speaking things desired into existence. Being formed in God's image allows mankind to have a personality for fellowship with the Creator.

Frederick K. C. Price: *Three Keys to Positive Confession*

You control God's power in your life with your words. You control your destiny. You are the captain of your own ship.[21]

Truth: How can a mere man control God's power in his life with his words? The LORD does as He pleases (Daniel 4:35). He is the potter and we are the clay (Isaiah 64:8). For a Holy Spirit-led life, we depend on the LORD (Proverbs 3:5-6) because He knows the future. Jesus is to have pre-eminence (Colossians 1:18) in our life, and be the captain of our ship according to His Holy Spirit-led destiny.

Bill Winston: *The Law of Confession*

The law of confession is one of the basic, fundamental laws that govern this universe and determine our destiny.... There is nothing in the universe so big and so powerful that it cannot be turned around with your tongue.[22]

Truth: If you look at the various verses where "confession" is used, you will not find one verse teaching there is a "law of confession" that God uses to govern *His* universe. He upholds and controls all things by word of *His* power (Hebrews 1:3). To say and believe that our tongue has the power to turn around the universe is to move the LORD off of *His* throne and seat ourselves on the throne. Didn't another deceived being have a similar idea in mind? (Isaiah 14:12-15). Was he successful?

Winston: Studying the law of confession also brings us into a new understanding of time. We are to be like God, and He lives outside of time.... There is no time in the spirit; therefore God can override time, and so can you and I.... You have been designed to use the law of confession to override time.[23]

Truth: Mr. Winston continues to add unbiblical ideas to the Christian lifestyle description, and conjures up what Christians can do supernaturally with a law of confession that God has not instituted. No verse teaches Christians are designed to use "the law of confession to override time." Believing false teachings does not redeem our time wisely (Ephesians 5:15-17).

Winston: We know the law of confession is true for the saved and the unsaved alike because confession is a law. When an unbeliever says something they believe, it comes to pass.[24]

Truth: The Word of God doesn't record such absurdity. If this teaching were true, and it is *not*, then atheists and demon-indwelled witches could use Holy Spirit power for miracles. God doesn't bless the unsaved with Holy Spirit miracles from their mouth while they continually blaspheme His Name and reject His grace (Ephesians 2:8-9).

Winston: Neither God nor the devil can do anything without your permission.[25]

Truth: This law of confession belief teaches that our words control both Satan and God. Ephesians 3:20 declares otherwise, and Psalm 12:4 describes the tongue of sin: "Who have said, With our tongue will we prevail; our lips are our own: who is lord over us?" The Christian mouth is not lord; Jesus is LORD!

These quotes establish that strong and unwavering *faith in spoken words*, attached to Scripture, is taught as the main focus in "positive confession." Thus, it is obvious why some people say they are "Word of Faith" or "Word-Faith" believers. They believe faith in a selected verse, mixed with faith in *their* spoken or confessed words *requires* God to give them what they speak. Such a belief gives *their* spoken words priority over God's will. This is sin (self-focus and word idolatry), and is *not* the true word of faith taught in Romans 10:8. The Scriptures are filled with examples of God's servants praying, asking, or calling upon Him as examples for us to follow in obedience.

Also, if these "positive confession people" really believe God must support their positive faith confessions, then where were they when Hurricane Katrina demolished the Gulf Coast in 2005? And where were they in 2012 when Hurricane Sandy blasted the East Coast? They had plenty of time to prepare with fasting and prayer. They could have gathered "positive confession believers" from Louisiana, Arkansas, Oklahoma, and Texas. These states contain numerous faith teaching churches that teach "Faith can do miracles." Then "By faith," hundreds of them could have lined the Gulf Coast and the East Coast and commanded the hurricanes to become a coastal breeze.

So where were they? Did they not have enough combined faith to "confess and declare" a calm miracle of nature? Or did they know *their* "positive confession" belief was comprised of words that God does not honor? The Almighty God controls the nature He made, not man's mouth (Proverbs 30:4).

On May 20th, 2013, a huge, vicious tornado devastated Moore, Oklahoma. It came with winds in excess of 200 mph and was at least a mile wide at times. The physical destruction was unbelievable, and 24 people were killed and more than 300 were injured. Why am I mentioning this? If these Word of Faith people really believe *their* bridled tongues with words of faith power can command the course of nature, *where were they when the tornado* was on its way to Moore, Oklahoma? They have taught for decades that Christians can do great miracles like Jesus did. Why didn't they fast and pray in advance, then confess and command the tornado to unwind itself and become a calm wind just as Jesus calmed the stormy sea in Matthew 8:23-27?

Oklahoma and Texas have violent storm problems every year. Parts of these states are located in a path called Tornado Alley where numerous twisters/tornados have come through annually for years. So why haven't the Word-Faith believers "practiced dismantling" small tornados to increase their faith to bridle and command anything violent in nature to obey their words? *Their* powerless faith talk and false teachings are evident.

Some false faith preachers say, "Satan is behind all of nature's catastrophes" and "We have power over Satan and his demons." If both quoted teachings in the previous sentence are true, why haven't the Word-Faith believers rebuked the numerous "demonic" tornados, torrential downpours, and untimely droughts that have brought immense loss and suffering to The United States of America? Are they afraid to go public with *their* faith to face tornados?

They talk about mountain-moving faith, but I have not heard of one faith-emphasizing preacher who has had success in dealing with God's nature like Jesus. Faith that is not backed by love/charity and truth is *nothing* as taught in 1 Corinthians 13:2. For those who prayed, wept, donated money, items of need, time, and talent to help the thousands who suffered any type of loss from this tornado and other catastrophes, may "the LORD'S most abundant blessings of His choice" be with you in this world and the heavenly world to come. Truly, all of you displayed the love of the real Jesus.

Occult Links to "Positive Confession"

The unbiblical concept of word power is brought out in an article titled *Speaking Your Intention Gives it More Power*. The author mentions his involvement with the Law of Attraction, a law commonly used in the occult. He mentions three areas that deserve our attention:

1. Words have power. Thoughts have power too but it is very important to take care of what you say, for you shall have what you say.

2. You can literally speak things into life…. The tongue controls life and death.

3. The throat chakra is the center of the will expression. You express your will into the world by the words you speak.

Look back at #1. It ends with the words "for you shall have what you say." This is the same meaning as "You can have what you say." The occult consistently recognizes and teaches the power of words. True Christianity consistently recognizes and teaches the power of the Word of God made flesh (John 1:1-3, 14).

Teaching #2 sounds just like the "You can have what you say" followers who use "word-confession." They pursue the road of manifestation through "verbal confessions." In the occult it's called "affirmations." Their tongue is lord over what they say (Psalm 12:4), so why listen to the Lord Jesus?

Teaching #3 mentions the throat chakra being the center of the will expression. For those who have detailed understanding about "chakra energy," the serious implications of this occult teaching are clear. Occult chakra teachings are found in witchcraft and Kundalini Yoga. The occult has many teachings about the 7 chakras from the lower spine to the top of the head. When you get involved with "chakra energy," you definitely open the demonic door to your life! The will of expression should be words expressing God's will in our lives, not our will (Matthew 6:10).

Notice that this teaching says "the throat chakra is the center of the will expression," and one's will is spoken from the throat with words. Your spoken word of will (what you say or confess) is another way of saying "You can have what you say" according to faith in your spoken words.[26]

Author Ann Fischer is a psychic, clairvoyant, and Metaphysician. Inside the front jacket cover of her book *Omni-Cosmics: Miracle Power Beyond the Subconscious* she states, "Whatever You Desire

You Can Have!" On page 147 she writes, "You will have all you want. Set it in your mind. It will come to pass! **Decree Positive Commands And They Will Come To Pass**." (bold in original).

In her book, she instructs the reader how to direct the Universal Mind (an occult name for God) to reach into the Universe and do as directed according to one's decrees that control spirits. She admits to becoming "engrossed with the occult" (page 6), and writes Omni-Cosmic rituals are the "power of the universe" (page 7). She also says "Your positive commands produce the wealth you so desire."[27]

These two occult sources show an obvious evil link with what some call biblical "positive confession." This revealing information should not be ignored and tossed aside as trivial. Why? Because it teaches there is supernatural occult power which transpires through "spoken words" and "decrees" that is *not* from the Holy Spirit! We are to "cast off the works of darkness" (Romans 13:12).

From the numerous false "positive confession" quotes in this chapter that were compared to Scripture and analyzed, it is very clear that anyone who professes to be a Christian should abstain from "positive confession." A fruitful and abundant life relationship with our Lord and Savior is one that continues in prayer (Philippians 4:6; Colossians 4:2; 1 Thessalonians 5:17), not "positive confession."

For those who teach Christians can speak "affirmations" with prayer, you will not find one Bible verse where Jesus used the word "affirmation" when teaching on prayer. Jesus does not want Christians imitating Satan's spiritual ways. He taught us to pray, ask (Matthew 6:9-13; John 14:13-14), and "come boldly unto the throne of grace, that we may obtain mercy, and find grace to help in the time of need" (Hebrews 4:15-16).

Also, please don't replace prayer or add to it with "declarations" or "decrees" of what you want. You are *not* God. Let the LORD decree how He wants to bless you. Come in submission and put your requests before Him. Pray, be thankful, and patient (1 John 5:14-15).

Is Positive Confession Pleasing to God?

Beware of those who say "I'm going to pray for you" but don't pray. Instead they *declare/confess* healing, favor, prosperity, success, or whatever they conjure up. Such a person is not praying to God on your behalf, but is "impersonating God" by being presumptuous about God's will for you in areas of your life. These God-impersonators continue to gain acceptance on Christian networks.

Please remember, Christians need to take a careful look at how and why they "claim" verses for a specific purpose. Claiming Bible verses improperly is sinful and can result in worshipping the written Word rather than Jesus, the living Word. Incorrect use of Bible verses describes the ongoing sin of "positive confession people." They have a *more* personal relationship with Bible verses (biblical idolatry), rather than a proper personal relationship with the Lord Jesus.

Christians have a responsibility to be of a sober spirit for the purpose of prayer (1 Peter 4:7). Positive confession is not sound judgment and *restrains* spiritual soberness. It is intoxicated with error and has no biblical purpose pertaining to prayer. If you have been deceived concerning "positive confession," the real Jesus is waiting to hear your confession prayer of repentance. He will forgive you.

Look back at the chapter title. That question has been answered by evaluating Scripture in proper context. Our Lord Jesus *never* used "positive confession" when teaching us to pray, request, do miracles, ask, or call upon His Father for anything. True Christians will not use "positive confession" for health, wealth, or anything. It's unbiblical.

Endnotes:

1. Kenneth E. Hagin, *"You Can Have What You Say!"* (Tulsa, Oklahoma: Rhema Bible Church, 1979), pp. 1-6.
2. W. E. Vine, *An Expository Dictionary Of New Testament Words* (Old Tappan, New Jersey: Fleming H. Revell Company, 1966), pp. 224, 225.
3. Ibid., p. 225.
4. Charles Capps, *The Tongue—A Creative Force* (England, Arkansas: Capps Publishing, 1995), p. 1.

5. Ibid., pp. 74, 75.

6. Charles Capps, *Faith and Confession* (England, Arkansas: Capps Publishing, 1987), p. 78.

7. Ibid., pp. 134-135.

8. Ibid., p. 211.

9. Ibid., p. 213.

10. Ibid., p. 244.

11. Dr. David Yonggi Cho, *The Fourth Dimension Volume One* (Alachua, Florida: Bridge-Logos Publishers, 1979), p. 64.

12. Ibid., p. 68.

13. Gloria Copeland, *God's Will is Prosperity* (Fort Worth, Texas: Kenneth Copeland Publications, 1978), p. 109.

14. Dr. Creflo A. Dollar Jr., *The Image of Righteousness You're More Than You Know* (Tulsa, Ok: Harrison House Inc., 2002), p. 87.

15. E. W. Kenyon & Don Gossett, *Speak Life* (New Kensington, PA: Whitaker House, 2013), p. 259.

16. T. L. Osborn, *Healing The Sick A Living Classic* (Tulsa, OK: Harrison House Inc., 1992), p.118.

17. Ibid., p. 121.

18. Ibid., p. 137.

19. John Osteen, *There is a Miracle in Your Mouth* (Houston, Texas: Lakewood Church, 1972), pp. 42-43.

20. Rod Parsley, *Your Harvest is Come* (Columbus, Ohio: Results Publishing, 1999), p. 47.

21. Frederick K. C. Price, *Three Keys to Positive Confession* (Los Angeles, CA: Faith One Publishing, 1994), p. 54.

22. Dr. Bill Winston, *The Law of Confession* (Tulsa, Oklahoma: Harrison House Publishers, 2009), pp. viii, ix.

23. Ibid., pp. 9, 11, 12.

24. Ibid., p. 37.

25. Ibid., p. 43.

26. http://www.mindreality.com/speaking-your-intention-gives-it-more-power

27. Ann Fischer, *Omni-Cosmics: Miracle Power Beyond the Subconscious* (West Nyack, New York: Parker Publishing Company Inc., 1979), p. 122.

Chapter 6

Four Steps to Health and Wealth?

In a booklet titled *How to Write Your Own Ticket With God*,[1] author Kenneth E. Hagin writes that Jesus appeared to him and gave him a 4-step formula (4 principles of operation) for always receiving whatever a Christian wants from Him, or from His Father. Supposedly this 4-step verbal teaching came in a vision directly from Jesus. The 4 steps Jesus taught to Kenneth Hagin for health and wealth are taken from Mark 5:25-34. This section of Scripture is also referred to as "garment touching faith healing" by some. Faith-entrenched people are convinced this area of Scripture, "if done by faith," entitles them to receive healing and money.

Let's test this vision teaching from the Jesus who appeared to Kenneth Hagin and see if it contradicts Scripture in any areas. If any contradiction is found, then *we will know* the real Jesus didn't appear to Kenneth Hagin with this 4-step teaching.

Mr. Hagin says this vision and verbal exchange occurred in Phoenix, Arizona, (December, 1953) after a service when people decided to pray (pages 2-3). When this Jesus appeared to him, no one else seemed to be aware of a dramatic event that was taking place. During the vision, Pastor Hagin was told to get a pencil and Jesus explained a 4-step formula that was found in Mark 5:25-34, and told him whenever these 4 steps (principles) were followed, people could always receive healing, finances, and victory. By comparing the evidence in Mark 5:25-34 with what this "vision Jesus" taught Mr. Hagin (pages 7-16), we can see if it is the *same* teaching that Jesus of Nazareth taught 2,000 years ago when healing the woman with the bleeding problem.

In verses 25-28, a woman with a blood issue of twelve years touched the garment of Jesus and said, "If I may touch but His clothes,

I shall be whole." She is healed, and Jesus acknowledges her faith brought healing and tells her to go in peace (verse 34). Though she receives healing, Jesus does not take time to teach 4-step "garment touching faith healing." If this is what truly manifested the woman's healing and this healing was for all, what kept the real Jesus from teaching the entire crowd about it? Another instance of people touching the hem of His garment and receiving healing is documented in Matthew 14:34-36, and no "4 principles of operation" for healing or "garment touching faith healing" were taught by the real Jesus.

The Jesus who appeared to this preacher said the 4 steps for healing that were found in Mark 5:25-34 were also found in 1 Samuel 17 where the fight between David and Goliath is recorded. Here are the 4 steps this vision Jesus spoke and gave to Kenneth Hagin as proof of these principles from Scripture. Mr. Hagin said Jesus told him to write 1, 2, 3, 4. Let's look at the Mark 5:25-34 setting, and learn about this 4-step *vision* teaching.

> **Step 1**: Say it. According to what the individual says, that shall he receive (pages 6-8).

> **Step 2**: Do it. According to your action, you receive or you are kept from receiving (page 11).

> **Step 3**: Receive it (page 12).

> **Step 4**: Tell it so others may believe (page 19).

The sequence of these 4 steps (principles) from *How to Write Your Own Ticket With God* for health and wealth, which supposedly came from the real Jesus, will now be given a Scripture test to see *if* they line up with the inspired Word of God (2 Timothy 3:16). If these 4 steps are not found in Scripture, we must reject them.

Four Steps to Health and Wealth?

Step 1: "Say it" is said by the woman in Mark 5:28.

Step 2: "Do it" requires faith in action, which implies a *physical* action of obedience to fulfill this step of faith. The woman did this as she walked up and touched Jesus. But what if a person is in a wheel chair or can't get out of a hospital bed? Wouldn't the healing need to take place *before* the person could get up? Step 2 does not make sense because it requires the disabled person to "Do it" before the healing occurs. When healing, Jesus did not tell the multitudes to "Do it" to receive their healing. He was the One "doing it" for them.

Step 3: The woman did receive her healing according to her faith as directed by God, but it *does not prove* this was the real Jesus 1,900 years later, who was "vision talking" to this preacher about Mark 5:25-34. In this setting, His Father wanted that one specific woman to receive her healing. There was a multitude around Him (verse 31), and many had crowded and pressed upon Him. Also, since Jesus is no longer passing by us daily, how do we touch His garment for healing as some still teach?

Step 4: We tell others so they may believe. What do we tell them? Do we say we have a 4-step formula for health and wealth that the Lord Jesus didn't even teach His apostles, a teaching that is not found in *The Book of Acts* or any epistles?

Are we to believe that Jesus let His followers suffer and miss out on God's health and wealth for over 1,900 years, and then appear to just one man in a vision that no one else saw and give him this 4-step health and wealth special teaching? If this is the real Jesus Who appeared to Mr. Hagin, why did He wait several centuries to reveal such an important teaching if it could have been helping millions of Christians since His heavenly ascension?

Let's break down the David and Goliath encounter to see if this 4-step formula is found 1 Samuel 17, as taught by this spiritual being who claimed to be the real Jesus. Mr. Hagin said Jesus told him David used the same 4 steps of faith found in Mark 5:25-34 to kill Goliath (page 21). If this is true, what kept David or the LORD, Who talked audibly to the prophets and kings, from telling all of Israel about these 4 steps after Goliath was slain? When you study the historical difficulties and sufferings of Israel, any supernatural type of help would have been welcomed, especially a 4-step faith formula for every person to use as needed. Now, the David and Goliath 4-step test.

Step 1: David does "Say it." He is convinced he can defeat Goliath (verses 45-47).

Step 2: David does "Do it" on the battlefield as he kills Goliath with his sling and a stone (verses 49-51).

Step 3: This "vision Jesus" said in this step we receive what we have said in faith. The battle ended in step 2. David's faith had brought victory for Israel. Goliath was dead before step 3. There is no reason for continuing on to step 3 or 4. This teaching was from a "vision Jesus," and was supposed to verify the context of Mark 5:25-34. All it did was verify that this was *not* the real Lord Jesus who appeared to Pastor Hagin. Also, David's victory was *not* a miracle that fits accurately into the 4-step miraculous formula. It was an act of courage.

Furthermore, the real Jesus Who taught and encouraged constant prayer would not appear about 1,900 years after His heavenly ascension to teach a 4-step formula for miracles and healings that contradicts 1 Corinthians 12:9-11. The Bible repeatedly teaches prayer (Acts 13:3; Ephesians 6:18; Philippians 4:6; Colossians 4:2; 1 Thessalonians 5:17; James 5:13-18; 1 John 5:14-15), not 4-step principles for getting what you want.

An additional shocking comment this "vision Jesus" said to the preacher was that if Christians did not use these 4 steps to achieve "victory over the world, the flesh and the devil" then the victory they desired would not come to pass, and "it would be a waste of their time to pray for Jesus to give them the victory" (page 20). When compared with Scripture, Kenneth E. Hagin's claim that Jesus appeared to him does not pass the test. It was "another Jesus" (2 Corinthians 11:4).

Popular Verses Used for Health and Wealth

Mark 9:17-30 reveals that a stubborn demon had been in a boy since he was child (verse 21). The disciples were not able to cast it out (verse 18) and the father appealed to Jesus seeking His compassion and help (verse 22). In verse 23 Jesus says to the man, "If thou canst believe, all things are possible to him that believeth." Then Jesus casts the demon out. "Positive confession" people teach that when Jesus said "all things are possible to him who believes" Jesus meant, "Whatever you believe by faith (health or wealth) makes all things possible with God." Is this really what Jesus is teaching at this demonic situation?

Jesus was talking to the father, not the entire multitude that had gathered (verses 16-17). The words "you" and "him" in verse 23 verify Jesus is speaking directly to this man and no one else. In this situation Jesus did not say, "All things are possible to *anyone* who claims this Scripture for health and wealth in the future and believes." Nor did Jesus say "All things are *guaranteed* to anyone who believes in Me." Remember, Jesus always did what His Father wanted, not always what man wanted (John 4:34; 5:19-20; 6:38; 8:29).

By definition, the word "guarantee" conveys assurance or promise, sometimes in writing on a document. The word "possible" conveys something may be, or can be; not absolute for sure. Examples of where the word "possible" is used are found in Acts 20:16 and Romans 12:18. These two verses show that when the word "possible" is used, it does not mean what is possible with God *guarantees* our desired results. Along with Mark 9:23, these two examples show when the word "possible" is used, it means in accordance with God's will (1 John 5:14) and/or one's effort. There is no guaranteed health and wealth for all in Mark 9:23.

Jesus is focusing *only* on this man's request and belief at this time. The sentence structure makes it clear that Jesus did not intend to turn this conversation with one person into a new doctrine of, "All things are possible to as many who believe for what they want in any situation." If the Lord wanted to teach "positive confession" to this huge crowd and explain that "all things are possible to any who believe," then the scene was set for this confession teaching. But Jesus did not teach "faith confession" after rebuking the demon. Instead, He went to a house, talked to His disciples, then departed, and went through Galilee (verses 28-30).

When the context of Mark 9:17-30 is examined, there is no reason to believe the words of Jesus *guarantee* "We can have what we say because all things are possible through faith with positive confession." The focus of belief and faith in this demonic setting rests on what was possible with the authority of Jesus concerning *this man's* request. This man sought the Lord's help, which all humble and submissive Christians should always do.

Another verse used incorrectly by Word of Faith ministers is Romans 10:9. It teaches if you confess Jesus as Lord and believe God has raised Him from the dead, you shall be saved. Salvation is the context of this verse, but some teach this verse also represents physical healing. They say the Greek word "saved" (*sōzō*) used in this verse, means that both salvation and physical healing are guaranteed when we receive Christ as our Savior. *Strong's Concordance* provides us with this definition of *sōzō*: "to save, i.e. deliver or protect (lit.or fig.): heal, preserve, save (self), do well, be (make) whole."[2] So this word (*sōzō*) can refer to salvation or healing.

However, the context of how *sōzō* is used determines the proper understanding of what Paul communicates in this verse. What is Paul's concern in verse 9? His concern is for those who need Christ's forgiveness that leads to salvation, and there is no emphasis on guaranteed physical healing in verse 10.

Romans 10:1 records Paul's prayer for Israel's salvation. He continues on to verse 9 and *never* talks about asking God for their physical healings. Nowhere in this chapter does the apostle Paul plead for the Jews to be spiritually forgiven *and* physically healed.

Clearly, Romans, chapter 10, is about people being saved from their sins by believing in Jesus as the Christ (Messiah). Those who teach that Romans 10:9 *guarantees* both salvation and healing to all, who with faith "confess" this Scripture and call upon the LORD for healing, are misrepresenting this verse. The unlearned and unstable distort verses like Romans 10:9, causing deception (2 Peter 3:16). We need to be stabilized in truth, not being "tossed to and fro, and carried about with every wind of doctrine" (Ephesians 4:14).

God's will for all is found in 2 Peter 3:9, and it's not guaranteed health and wealth. For any who desire His forgiveness, He has freely given them the opportunity to receive His salvation and avoid the consequences of sin (John 1:12; 3:16). The LORD'S will is for all to be saved (1 Timothy 2:4). Nowhere in the teachings of Jesus and His disciples is it written that "God's will is to heal and financially prosper all" who become Christians.

Are Word of Faith Televangelists Misleading Millions?

Tragically, Christian television continues to allow numerous false faith preaching men and women to present their personal Scriptural formulas from "heavenly visions" on health, wealth, and miracles. Such ministers of deception are often featured as special guests on Christian talk shows. They sell their books and visual aids. They declare if you purchase their product, you will receive healing and prosperity *if* you apply "with faith" their steps for activating the blessings of God. Beware of Sid Roth's telecast: *It's Supernatural.*

If you study all of the healings Jesus and His disciples did in the Gospels and *Book of Acts,* you will find that no 4-step formulas for healing were taught to the many who were healed. Stay away from any teachings that guarantee health and wealth for all if you follow a certain step-by-step process or formula, because they are not from the Holy Spirit. They are unbiblical.

Endnotes:
1. Kenneth E. Hagin, *How to Write Your Own Ticket With God* (Tulsa. OK: Kenneth Hagin Ministries, 1979).
2. James Strong, *Strong's Exhaustive Concordance of the Bible* (Nashville, Tennessee: Abingdon Press, 1976), p. 70.

Chapter 7

Analyzing Quantum Faith

Within the last ten years, a new faith teaching called "quantum faith" has gained acceptance and spread throughout faith teaching ministries. Quantum faith is linked with quantum physics, which studies atoms and small subatomic particles (quarks, gluons), their movement, and how they react to sound. Faith-focused people are convinced the sound of their words can move the elements of nature and this makes the elements obey *their* "words of faith." Then quantum miracles occur. But does the Bible confirm such a teaching as the work of the Holy Spirit?

Is it possible that "quantum faith" has an occult connection? Several quotes from Annette Capps, daughter of the late Charles Capps, will be listed to show the unbiblical foundation of "quantum faith."

Annette Capps: *Quantum Faith*[1]

> Before God spoke and said "Let there be light," the substance for light was there. The sound vibration of His words caused the substance to manifest and appear (page 7).

Truth: No verse teaches God needed any substance *before* His creation of light so that He could create light. Also, a careful reading of Genesis 1-2 will verify that the LORD did not use the sound vibration of His words to cause light to manifest and appear. Word vibration teachings are found in occult New Age and mystical belief, not in God's creation of all things.

> Words are energy and energy affects matter.... Your words are energy and they affect matter in your life.... The substance from which our world is made is influenced and manifested by words. The things you desire are made up of atoms. They know

what you believe, hear what you say and behave accordingly (pages 7, 9).

Truth: To teach that atoms have knowledge which enables them to know what we believe, hear what we say, and then respond accordingly to our words is *not* taught in Scripture. Such a belief puts man on God's throne in place of Him for the purpose of ruling over the elements of His nature. Our Lord Jesus controls/upholds *all things* by word of His power (Hebrews 1:3). He is Lord of creation (John 1:1-3; Colossians 1:16-17), not any mystical demon or any human!

When Jesus spoke to the fig tree and said, "No man eat fruit from thee hereafter forever," then that fig tree dried up from the atomic level because of His words. When He spoke to the winds and the waves, they obeyed Him. He was teaching us the undeniable Biblical principle that *THINGS OBEY WORDS* (page 11).

Truth: Yes, all created matter (things) does obey the words of its Creator (Genesis 1:1-27; Proverbs 30:4), not because it has intelligence, but because the Creator has all authority over His particles of creation. Jesus spoke miraculous words, and they supernaturally changed the created matter of nature because it was His Father's will (John 5:19-20; 8:29). And no one can do a Holy Spirit miracle unless it is God's will (1 Corinthians 12:10-11).

All "things" respond to the vibration of energy.... You have a choice to use the energy of your words to change matter. The things in your life will obey your words. By speaking to objects such as your computer, "Stupid computer! It's going to crash!" you will find that it obeys you (page 14).

Truth: Where is the Bible verse that teaches the "vibration energy" of our words changes matter of any kind according to our will? Jesus didn't teach "the things in life will obey your words." And talking to our computer believing it has "quantum subatomic intelligence" that must obey our spoken word is not taught in Scripture.

Imagine taking the highest frequency of all, the vibrating creative words of God, and changing the vibration of those "things" you want changed! (page 15).
Truth: Look through your concordance and you will see that the Holy Spirit did not move any writer to mention God's high frequency of creative words. Miss Capps continues to lure people into thinking they can change what they want with their words of choice. Has she forgotten about the numerous verses and examples of prayer to God for His will to be done? (1 John 5:14-15). The LORD'S Word changes things, not our word.

Faith is an unseen energy force. It is not matter, but it creates matter and actually becomes matter.... Faith is the raw material from which all matter is made (page 22).
Truth: In Hebrews 11, faith is not taught as "an unseen energy force." No verse says "it creates matter and actually becomes matter." The energy seen as examples of faith in this chapter is the energy of obedience from individuals who obeyed God to prove their faith. It is ridiculous to believe that faith is a "raw material from which all matter is made." Before the beginning, there was no physical matter yet created, and out of nothing (Hebrews 11:3) the LORD created the heavens and the earth.

He spoke and the vibration (sound) of his words released the substance that became the stars and planets.... Just as God created the universe by faith-substance and word-energy, you create your own universe by faith and your words. If you don't like what you have created, you can change it! (pages 22, 23).
Truth: It is shocking to see this unbiblical information describing the Almighty Creator of the Universe as a God Who supposedly used "word-energy and vibrating faith-substance" to bring the Universe into existence. This description of the

Creator sounds more like a New Age-mystical god. Not one creation Scripture from Genesis to Revelation matches the identity of Annette Capp's definition of her creator. No sound-minded person who knows the Bible would ever believe, "By faith and my words, I can create my universe." If this were true, then why pray and who needs God?

How you interact with this quantum field of possibilities, the unseen realm from which all is created, determines what manifests in your life (page 24).

Truth: Jesus and His disciples taught us how to react with the unseen realm so that we would see God's manifested will in our lives. It was through rejoicing, prayer, thanksgiving, and obedience to God (Matthew 6:9-13; John 14:13; Romans 12:12; Philippians 4:4-7; Colossians 4:2; 1 Thessalonians 5:16-18; 1 Peter 4:7; Jude 20). Without knowledge of quantum physics or quantum faith, the early Body of Christ did quite well in obedience to Matthew 28:19 and Acts 1:8.

The 2010 edition of her book says more than 100,000 have been sold. Quantum faith is not true Holy Spirit faith, as some "quantum sources" will now confirm.

The Quantum Faith/Quantum Physics Power Source

These sources will show that those who use "quantum faith" to make miraculous things happen in the quantum physics realm are not being helped by God's Holy Spirit, but are getting help from evil spirits.

The spelling with a "k" will refer to the occult sciences.... I can tell you that the same basic principles of the Law of Attraction are the basic principles of magick.... Similarly, Law of Attraction is based on energy frequencies and higher levels of energy focused through the visualization of the desire.... The Law of Attraction works like magic because it is magick....

And quantum physics is providing the scientific, empirical evidence that sorcerers, wizards, and witches have worked with for centuries.[2]

Insight: This source says the Law of Attraction is rooted in magick (when magic is spelled with a "k," it refers to the occult, witchcraft, and demon activity). It also states that what is now called quantum physics has been used by *sorcerers, wizards, and witches* for centuries. There is no mention in the Gospels of the Lord Jesus using this power for miracles, because this power realm is found in the occult where Satan and his evil spirits do their magickal work to deceive people.

An article by Kate Corbin says *The Law of Attraction and Quantum Physics* sums up best what New Age converts tout as proof of man's inherit powers. Corbin writes, "The Law of Attraction teaches that we attract into our lives whatever we focus on. Quantum physics teaches that nothing is fixed, that there are no limitations, and that everything is vibrating Energy. By understanding that everything is Energy in a state of potential and by applying the Law of Attraction to bring into our lives what we focus on, it is never necessary to feel stuck with an undesirable life.... We are Creators of the Universe.[3]

Insight: Again we have a teaching connecting the Law of Attraction (an occult law) with the vibrating energy of quantum physics. Christians should never use an occult teaching for any purpose, because it opens the door for demonic influence.

From a teaching called *What Is Real Magick*? Magick is another word for transformation, creation, and manifestation. Wicca magick is a tool we use to act on the subtle—or energy, or quantum—level of reality. The quantum level is the **causal realm**. It is the subtle influences at the quantum level that decide which way reality will go. **So if you want to manifest something into ordinary reality, you start by stimulating the quantum realm to favour that potentiality.** That is real magick in action…. In magick we transform our reality, and ourselves, to match our choices.[4] (Creative Visualization?).

Insight: This information reveals that magick (witchcraft power) is the source stimulating the quantum realm that causes manifestations to occur. If people, who call themselves Christians, are using the quantum realm or level to get miracles or anything to manifest, they need to stop and renounce all involvement with this blatant witchcraft/Wicca teaching. If you are a Christian, spend more time in prayer and fasting to receive guidance from the Lord, rather than speaking words that might activate demons from the quantum realm. If you truly love Jesus, don't mess with the occult, unless you prefer fellowship with demons.

The Laws of Quantum Physics tells us that there exists an infinite ocean of thinking, intelligent energy called the Quantum Ocean. This is the Mind of God that the ancients spoke about…. The Quantum Ocean responds to our thoughts (page 1). The Laws of Quantum Physics tells us that the Laws of Attraction will bring you what you think about—Think about God and those Higher ones who have gone before, those who are higher on the mountain. They will hear you. (page 2). This information is from an article titled, *Quantum Physics and Spirituality.*[5]

Insight: The first sentence mentions intelligent energy in the Quantum Ocean, and then calls it the Mind of God. The mind of God is found in Christ the Lord, not in an ocean of subatomic particles. The Higher ones mentioned who will hear you are most likely demons who will hear you, connect with your thoughts, speak to your mind, and pull you into Spiritism. Again, the occult Law of Attraction is tied to quantum physics.

These sources should alert you to the occult nature of Quantum Physics, and its connection to the "quantum spiritual realm." Those who pursue "quantum faith" for the purpose of interacting with the quantum subatomic particles to bring forth manifestations from the spiritual to the physical realm should realize the manifestations are *not* from the Holy Spirit. Does Annette Capps truly realize what she is embracing and teaching?

Another "quantum faith" teaching needs to be refuted so you will know that some of these quantum believers are literal when they teach "subatomic particles contain intelligence and memory." Here is the content of their understanding taken from three Scriptures.

Joshua 24:27 says "This stone shall be for a witness unto us; for it hath heard all the words of the LORD which He spoke unto to us." Habakkuk 2:11 says "For the stone shall cry out of the wall, and the beam out of the timber shall answer it." Also, Jesus said in Luke 19:40 that "the stones would immediately cry out." These verses prove there is memory and intelligence contained in all matter. This includes the subatomic particles that comprise all the physical things created by God.

Insight: These three verses are *not literal*. They are metaphors to give descriptive and strong understanding to what is being taught. A metaphor is "the application of a word or phrase to an object or concept which it does not literally denote, in order to suggest comparison with another object or concept, as in "A mighty fortress is our God."[6] Another example of a metaphor is found in Psalm 91:4 where it describes God in this manner: "He shall cover thee with His feathers, and under His wings shall thou trust." If we take this description of God literally, then we must conclude that the LORD is a bird with wings, yet we know this is not a literal description of God, for "God is Spirit" (John 4:24). This verse describes metaphorically how He watches over us as we seek comfort and refuge under His covering of love and protection. For those who believe matter contains intelligence, there is some truth to that belief. Digital technology has various memory chips for computers and phones. However, there is no verifiable scientific proof that the elements used for computer chips *always* had independent will with intelligence *before* people made the chip and loaded information into the chip or memory card. Genesis 1:20-31 describes the LORD'S creation of all living creatures. We know creature intelligence varies. Genesis 1 does not say the LORD created intelligence within the rocks or small subatomic particles. Thus, those who imply or teach otherwise are not respecting God's creation account in Genesis 1. We are given permission to rule over the living creatures (Genesis 1:26), but nothing is said about us ruling over inanimate matter, such as atoms and subatomic particles with "quantum faith."

There is no need to be involved with "quantum faith" because it has roots in occult-mystical faith, and has nothing in common with Holy Spirit faith. False quantum faith "offers sound" and depends on vibration, word energy, frequency, and the substance of energy from the elements of creation. True faith "offers prayer" and depends on God's indwelling Holy Spirit (Romans 8:9, 11), as He provides the needed spiritual energy.

If you are involved with any type of quantum faith practices, the information provided confirms it is unbiblical and wages war against a solid prayer life. Repent and fulfill 1 Thessalonians 5:16-18.

Endnotes:

1. Annette Capps, *Quantum Faith* (England, Arkansas: Capps Publishing, 2010).
2. http://ezinearticles.com/?Law-Of-Attraction-Is-Magick&id=538043
3. http://www.sacredpursuit.org/gpage57.html
4. http://www.wicca-spirituality.com/wicca-magick.html
5. http://ragnar111.wordpress.com/2008/05/23/quantum-physics-and-spirituality/
6. *Webster's Encyclopedic Unabridged Dictionary of the English Language* (New York, New York: Gramercy Books, 1996), p. 901.

Chapter 8

Bill Johnson and Bethel Church

Bill Johnson and his wife, Beni, are the senior leaders of Bethel Church in Redding, California. Strange spiritual encounters have been reported from Bethel Church. Unusual and personal beliefs will be cited in this chapter. These will be evaluated and compared to the Word of God.

A book titled *The Physics of Heaven* has caused great concern among many Christians because of the chapter contents presented by several writers. In chapter after chapter, authors Judy Franklin and Ellyn Davis present various unusual "supernatural" experiences from individuals who supposedly have had dynamic spiritual events transpire, which brought new thought and change in their lives.

On the back cover of this book, Judy Franklin is listed "on staff at Bethel Church in Redding, California." Ellyn Davis is recognized for her involvement in "the Christian home school market." The book I will quote from is the 2012 edition.[1] On the back cover it states this startling information:

> Ellyn has desire to bridge the gap between Christianity and the discoveries of quantum physics as well as discover God truths hidden in quantum mysticism.

Before opening her book, we are told that Ellyn Davis plans to "discover God truths hidden in quantum mysticism." So, does the Bible not contain all the truth we need to know? Does any verse in the Bible direct us to "discover God truths hidden" in another religion or spiritual realm? Isn't the Bible sufficient for all we need to know for abundant and eternal life? The spiritual realm of mysticism is eerie, strange, and evil. It is not the Holy Spirit realm of the LORD'S truth.

Are Word of Faith Televangelists Misleading Millions?

The following quotes from contributing people will show some unscriptural beliefs found in *The Physics of Heaven*. Scriptural comparison will be the standard of appraisal.

Judy Franklin:

> This book is just a precursor to the revelation that God is going to give us when He releases a new, transforming sound (page x).... The next thing the Lord told me was that soon He would release a sound from heaven that will literally change the structure of how we think. This new sound will transform us like the transformation spoken of in Romans 12. Our minds will be renewed so we think like Him and are no longer conformed to this world but conformed to the will of God. Bringing heaven to earth is our mandate, and to do that we need to think more like heaven (page 2).
>
> **Truth:** The Bible does not teach that Jesus will send a "sound" from heaven to change how we think. From the day we are born-again, we receive the Holy Spirit and He helps us change (renew) our mind and how we think (John 14:16-18, 26; 15:26; 16:13-14). And Jesus did not teach the apostles before He ascended to heaven that they were to bring heaven to earth.

> I decided to examine New Age thought and practice for anything "precious" that might be "extracted" from the worthless.... we are hearing more and more teaching about Christians "taking back truths" from the New Age that really belong to citizens of the Kingdom of God (page 15).
>
> **Truth:** The New Age is ongoing occultism. Why would our Lord put any of His precious truths in the kingdom of darkness? We have been delivered from the power and kingdom of darkness (Colossians 1:12-13), and are Saints of light! We are not directed by Scripture to go back into a New Age realm of sin looking for truth. All our needed truth is found from Genesis to Revelation. There is nothing to take back from the New Age, because the Word of God is always sufficient.

I believe that a great work of God is in process as He restores knowledge and insights that have been lost to Christians but are now hidden in the teachings and practices of Quantum Mysticism (page 17).

Truth: How would she know what was lost if the Bible doesn't tell what was lost, if anything at all? Would she guess, listen to her fleshly desires, place faith in New Age writings, or seek a spiritual voice? There are plenty of voices in the realm of Mysticism. His wisdom directs us to stay with the Bible, the written voice of God.

Jonathan Welton:

I have found throughout Scripture at least 75 examples of things that the New Age has counterfeited, such as having a spirit guide, trances, meditation, auras, power objects, clairvoyance, clairaudience, and more. These actually belong to the church, but they have been stolen and cleverly repackaged (page 49).

Truth: Jonathan Welton's "examples of things that the New Age has counterfeited" have nothing to do with the Holy Spirit power and gifts sent at Pentecost. There are nine gifts of the Holy Spirit mentioned in 1 Corinthians 12: 4-11, and more gifts are recorded in Romans 12:6-8. If you read these two sections of Scripture, you will realize that none of Mr. Welton's "examples of things" are mentioned as gifts of the Holy Spirit for the Body of Christ. And there is a reason why they are not listed as gifts of the Holy Spirit. All of the examples he cites are found in occult literature and are used by witches. I know this personally, because I have deceased relatives who were involved with the occult. Also, previous witches, who became Christians, told me about these common occult practices. And Jonathan Welton does not give any Scripture to prove how, and when these so-called gifts were stolen from the church. It is shocking that pastor Bill Johnson would allow his congregation to have information on various occult practices put in a book with him being one of the contributing writers.

Pastor Bill Johnson:

God is glorified by not speaking in plain language to you. He's glorified by speaking in parables, symbols and dark sayings (page 31).

Truth: Wrong Mr. Johnson. God is glorified in speaking plain language as found in John 1:12 and 14:6. He is the Lord of true light (John 1:4-5; 8:12). His language pulls people out of darkness.

You also see that Jesus healed every person who came to Him and turned no one away and that He is the exact representation of the Father (page 33).

Truth: Luke 5:15-16 says Jesus withdrew from multitudes who sought His healing. If He is the "exact representation" of the Father, then we must accept His will that all seeking healing will not be healed.

In 1995 I began to cry out to God every day and night for around eight months. My prayer was, "God, I want more of you at any cost! I will pay any price!" Then one night in October, God came to answer my prayer, yet not in a way I had expected. I went from being in a dead sleep to being wide-awake in a moment. Unexplainable power began to surge through my body. If I had been plugged into a wall socket with a thousand volts of electricity flowing through my body, I can't imagine that it would have been much different. It was as though an extremely powerful being had entered the room and I could not function in His presence. My arms and legs shot out in silent explosions as this power was released through my hands and feet. The more I tried to stop it, the worse it got.... I heard no voice, nor did I have any visions.... Several times throughout the ten years before this I had experienced the same kind of power in the middle of the night, but only in my legs, and much less in intensity. I did not know it was God. I had always thought something was wrong with my body.... This time, at 3:00 a. m., I knew it was.... I lay there with the realization that for the previous ten years God had been calling me to something new, something higher.... He had come to me on a mission. I was His target. It was a glorious experience, because it was Him. But it was not a very pleasant one. It was not gratifying in any natural sense.... I didn't know anyone who would believe that this was from God.... The power surges didn't stop. They continued throughout the night, with me weeping and praying, "More Lord, more, please give me more of you." Then it all stopped at 6:38 A. M. when I got out of bed completely refreshed. This experience continued the following two nights, beginning moments after getting into bed. When finished, I no longer thought the way I thought before. My mind had been completely transformed (pages 147-151).

Truth: Pastor Johnson's information details a very bizarre experience with what he describes as volts of electricity going through his body, and a presence he claims is God in his room. Is there any Scriptural proof to confirm this supernatural encounter was definitely the LORD God? Mr. Johnson states, "He had come to me on a mission." And what was the mission? Was it a mission of electricity with power surges that lasted over three hours? Two more nights of "mission electricity" and then pastor Johnson says, "My mind had been completely transformed." Is there any Scriptural evidence that the true God uses hour after hour of spiritual voltage for more than a day to transform just one mind? Jesus could do this instantly. There are *instant* miraculous Gospel accounts of the real Jesus quickly calming a storm, multiplying bread and fish, changing water to wine, raising the dead, and healing multitudes. If this was the real God of creation, what took Him so long to transform one mind? And years later, what is the fruit of this so-called visitation from God? Wasn't Bill Johnson renewing his mind daily like all spirit-filled Christians should be doing? (Romans 12:2; 2 Corinthians 4:16). And when you check Mr. Johnson's "electric" spiritual gifts doctrinal beliefs, do they conflict with the LORD'S Scripture?

From what pastor Johnson wrote, it is obvious that there was a supernatural presence in his room for hours during a three night span. However, when compared to the various visits to prophets and the apostles from the LORD that are found in the Bible, pastor Bill Johnson's spiritual encounter does not contain sufficient proof to verify that it was the real God Whose presence was in his room for three nights. And during these three "electric visitations" what was his wife doing or seeing?

Finally, did anything "electric" like this happen to Paul when the Lord Jesus got his attention with "a light from heaven" (Acts 9:3-16)? Did this "electric presence" inform pastor Johnson of a specific calling that was to glorify the LORD? (1 Corinthians 10:31).

A final piece of information should enlighten you to the Bethel quantum belief concerning the supernatural. It reads:

> All of the contributors to chapters in this book sense that God is on the verge of releasing something new on the earth and that new thing somehow involves vibrations, frequencies, energy, sound, light, and taking "quantum leaps" by faith (page 171).
> **Truth:** Those who contributed to *The Physics of Heaven* should realize God released vibrations, frequencies, energy, sound, and light during the first week of creation. So nothing new, according to Genesis 1, is coming in the "new thing" you are waiting to see released. Preach good messages on the Lord's return, and how He will bring in the true heavenly Kingdom with *His power* and His Holy angels. And perhaps you might consider a "quantum leap of repentance" by faith. Wasting time looking for God's truth hidden in quantum-

occult mysticism is a sin (Ephesians 5:15-17). Learn from Hebrews 11 about the faith that pleases the true God.

Do you remember the quantum occult connection information given in the previous chapter? It leads people to accept "dark sayings" as new lights of truth. The leadership at Bethel Church needs to close the door on delving into quantum mysticism for any kind of New Age insight that supposedly will provide a better understanding of God's truths. He has an abundance of truth for all in the Bible. It is an insult to the LORD God to say His Bible doesn't have all the truth we need.

Scientific study of quantum physics or how sound, light, energy, vibration, and frequencies impact creation does not offend the LORD of creation. It glorifies Him (Romans 1:20). But when you link occult ideas with the elements of His creation, and search for possible "God truths hidden in quantum mysticism" or occult New Age Thought, you have clearly disclosed that Jesus and the Bible are not good enough to satisfy a personal relationship with the Lord of truth (John 14:6).

Always remember: the Father, the Son, the Holy Spirit, and the Bible will meet our every need at all times.

Endnotes:
1. Judy Franklin & Ellyn Davis, *The Physics of Heaven* (Crossville, TN: Double Portion Publishing, 2012).

Hebrews, chapter 11

Now faith is the substance of things hoped for, the evidence of things not seen (verse 1).

But without faith it is impossible to please Him: for he that cometh to God must believe that He is, and that He is a rewarder of them that diligently seek Him (verse 6).

And others had trial of cruel mockings and scourgings, yea, moreover of bonds and imprisonment: They were stoned, they were sawn asunder, were tempted, were slain with the sword: they wandered about in sheepskins and goatskins; being destitute, afflicted, tormented; Of whom the world was not worthy: they wandered in deserts, and in mountains, and in dens and caves of the earth. And these all having obtained a good report through faith, received not the promise: God having provided some better thing for us, that they without us should not be made perfect (verses 36-40).

Chapter 9

Truth Establishes Biblical Faith

During the past forty years, there has been a huge increase in faith sermons, messages, and faith conferences around the world. Certain faith teachings are promoting "counterfeit faith." They are teaching people that when they have enough faith, then God will always give them their "faith declaration" or "faith confession." Misled faith preachers believe "Your faith controls and determines your destiny and circumstances" (success, favor, miraculous healings, and wealth are implied). This teaching requires God to serve people with strong faith, rather than people serving God with strong faith.

Hebrews 11 contains forty verses filled with vivid information describing faith in various situations. This chapter provides a true understanding of the biblical faith God desires to be evident in our daily lives (John 4:24). The Holy Spirit wants us to know what constitutes faith. Vine's *Expository Dictionary of New Testament Words* gives us insight about the word "faith" that pleases God:

> *PISTIS*, primarily, firm persuasion, a conviction based upon hearing ... is used in the N.T. always of faith in God or Christ or things spiritual ... The main elements in faith in its relation to the invisible God, as distinct from faith in man, are especially brought out in the use of this noun and the corresponding verb, *pistueō*; they are (1) a firm conviction, producing a full acknowledgement of God's revelation or truth, e. g., 2 Thess. 2:11, 12; (2) a personal surrender to Him, John 1:12; (3) a conduct inspired by such surrender, 2 Cor. 5:7. Prominence is given to one or other of these elements according to the context ... The object of Abraham's faith was not God's promise (that was the occasion of its exercise); his faith rested on God Himself, Rom. 4:17, 20, 21.[1]

Are Word of Faith Televangelists Misleading Millions?

Look again at the three areas of Vine's information on what is found in biblical faith. Belief and trust are implied partners with faith. When you have finished reading the information about faith in this chapter, you will *know* that many popular Word-Faith teachers contradict true biblical faith, because they *redefine* "faith."

Detailed study of the verses in Hebrews 11 makes it obvious that the people historically recognized did not "speak by faith," and declare their will to be done as the substance of their belief. The substance of their belief was obedient response to God's will when revealed personally, or through His messengers of choice. They followed God's spoken/written Word with confidence and assurance. God didn't follow their spoken word.

This is where false faith believers are deceived, because they insist if you have faith without doubt, God must honor your faith. No verse teaches the LORD is obligated to man's faith level (Isaiah 64:8). Our faith in God should accept His will for us whether or not it means health, success, and prosperity. Paul is an example of one who knew "both how to be abased ... how to abound ... to be full and to be hungry, both to abound and suffer need" (Philippians 4:12).

Numerous true faith examples show repeatedly that His servants had knowledge of His will, trusted, and obeyed Him. Where false faith followers create global "faith distortion" is found in their improper belief of verse 1 which reads:

> Now faith is the substance of things hoped for, the evidence of things not seen.

They believe faith is a spiritual substance Christians can speak and direct, and the "faith substance" of their belief will cause the LORD to give them the content of their words, such as healing and money. The Greek word for substance is *hupostasis* and translates: assurance, confidence, substance.[2] The definition of *hupostasis* in verse 1 does not teach we can use it to speak or proclaim health and wealth into our lives, and then God must respond to our unwavering faith of personal desire.

The writer of Hebrews 11 had the option from many verses to explain how to live a "faith for health and wealth" lifestyle as a Christian, if this was God's will. He didn't. Because when it comes to faith, our faith is demonstrated by how we obey or disobey the LORD, not according to how wealthy or healthy we are throughout our life.

In this section, I will list teachings from Word-Faith ministers to reveal how they misrepresent "faith" and "God" in Hebrews 11.

Charles Capps:

Here, essentially, is what God did. God filled His words with faith. He used His words as containers to hold His faith and contain that spiritual force and transport it out there into the vast darkness saying, *"Light, be!"* That's the way God transported His Faith causing creation and transformation.[3]

Truth: Genesis 1 does not say the LORD needed faith in His Word containers to create anything. None of this belief is found in the Bible. Mr. Capp's "faith imagination" is just that; a man's vain imagination (2 Corinthians 10:5).

Capps: *God releases sufficient faith in every word He speaks to cause it to come to pass.*[4]

Truth: Hebrews 11:3 doesn't teach God released "sufficient faith" in every word He spoke while creating the world.

Capps: Faith is a law also. You must have faith in the law of faith, and then make the law work by applying confession.[5]

Truth: There is no Scriptural law of faith that we use with confession of God's Word. Those who teach false doctrine reveal their lack of acceptance to the inspired Word of God (2 Timothy 3:16-17) by ignoring it or adding to it. Jesus said in Mark 11:22 we are to have faith in God, *not* in the law of faith!

Capps: *You must develop faith in your words so you can believe what you are saying day after day will come to pass.*[6]

Truth: Christian faith is in God, not our words (Mark 11:22).

Capps: Faith is *the* substance. It takes spiritual energy to bring the thing hoped for into manifestation. *The energy itself comes from the Word of God.*[7]

Truth: Spiritual energy is never used to describe the power of the Holy Spirit bringing things "hoped for into manifestation." The occult uses terms such as "spiritual energy" and "energy" in reference to manifesting the supernatural. To say the energy comes from the Word of God makes the Bible sound like it is an occult book used in conjuring up various spirits.

Capps: *Faith is the divine energy of God.*[8]

Truth: This belief insults the LORD, because it attributes an occult term (divine energy) as coming from God. No verse in the Bible supports this absurd teaching.

Capps: Genesis 1 is a copy of the words God used to release His faith.[9]

Truth: Nothing is said in Genesis 1 about God releasing His faith to create all things. The word "faith" is not found in Genesis 1. One wonders if Mr. Capps ever read Genesis 1 in a slow and careful manner, because he *adds* unbiblical words to God's Holy Word (Proverbs 30:5-6).

Gloria Copeland:

God called His will into substance by speaking words of faith. His words brought the material world into being.[10]

Truth: Genesis 1 does not teach that God spoke words of faith to bring this material world into being, nor does John 1:1-3 say anything about Jesus speaking words of faith to create matter. God does not need faith to do anything. He speaks and it happens (Isaiah 44:24; 45:12). Jeremiah 27:5 talks of the LORD'S great power, not His great faith.

Kenneth Copeland:

Faith is a power force. It is a conductive force.[11]

Truth: Mr. Copeland does not cite a verse to back up this teaching. Faith is never called "a force" in Hebrews 11.

Copeland: God is a faith being.[12]

Truth: The Almighty God is never called "a faith being." The Bible says God is love (1 John 4:8), and love is greater than faith (1 Corinthians 13:13). Focus on love (John 13:34-35).

Creflo Dollar:

We know God created all things by the power of His Word. Faith in His Word… When God spoke His words, they were filled with faith.[13]

Truth: Another Word-Faith minister who thinks the LORD needs faith in His Word to create. So did God meditate on His faith in eternity before He created the heavenly realm for the angels? And later, did He again have to meditate and check His faith level before He spoke the world into existence?

E. W. Kenyon:

God created the universe with words: faith-filled words.[14]

Truth: Mr. Kenyon (1867-1948) is wrong. "Faith-filled words" describing God's creation of the universe are *not* recorded in Genesis 1.

Kenneth E. Hagin:

Faith is always expressed in WORDS. Faith must be released in WORDS *through your mouth.*[15]

Truth: No verse supports Mr. Hagin's claim. Hebrews 11 clearly teaches that "By faith" people were obedient to God's will without using their mouth only. They did what He asked, and also used their bodies in obedience, showing that their faith was *not* "always expressed in words" from their mouth.

Andrew Wommack:

> Faith is governed by law.... There are laws that govern how healing works ... and how the power of God flows.[16]
>
> **Truth:** According to Hebrews 11, faith is not governed by law, and the Holy Spirit governs healing (1 Corinthians 12:9, 11).

These numerous unsound teachings just presented prove that misled Word-Faith preachers have derived their own definition of faith, one that is not found in Scripture. Their faith comes across as egotistical rather than submissive to the LORD. What's worse is that they reduce the eternal God to a person who needs faith to create. Thus, they have redefined the Almighty to their "faith preference." The next section will expose more deceptive unbiblical faith belief.

Have Faith in God or Have the Faith of God?

Many faith-focused people believe, teach, and declare that the words "Have faith in God" should be translated "Have the faith of God" in Mark 11:22. They say this proves God is a faith God and has to use faith to accomplish what He speaks, and as our faith gets stronger we too can speak miracles into existence. The "Have the faith of God" or "God kind of faith" doctrine is derived from this one verse.

To learn more about this controversial view of Mark 11:22, we need to look at the Greek structure in the verse. Renowned Greek scholar A. T. Robertson spent many years studying the Greek word structure in the New Testament. Robertson teaches the Greek for "Have faith in God" (*echete pistin theou*) is to be translated "Have faith in God," because of what is called an objective genitive in the Greek language.[17]

An objective genitive means that the noun (in this statement, *theou*) is the object of the action. Therefore, God is the object of faith in Mark 11:22. Your faith is *never* to be the object of your faith. To translate this verse "Have the faith of God" is to ignore the proper Greek translation guidelines, and place your faith in faith, which amounts to faith idolatry.

Concerning the objective genitive in Mark 11:22, R. C. H. Lenski also states:

> Mark reports this summary answer of Jesus in regard to what the dried-up fig tree teaches the disciples. They must go on having *pistis*, "faith," trust, complete reliance on God. *Theou* is the objective genitive, God is the object of the verbal idea contained in *pistis*.[18]

Again, the objective genitive is clarified, meaning that God is the object of true faith, *not* faith being the object of our faith. Word of Faith people also teach this verse can be translated, "Have the God kind of faith."

To reinforce this crucial truth of the correct translation, let's look at more Greek information from A. T. Robertson and W. Hersey Davis.

> But in *echete pistin Theou* (Mk.11:22) *have faith in God, Theou* is plainly the objective genitive, not the subjective. It is not the faith that God has, but the faith of which God is the object. In itself the case means only the God-kind of faith.[19]

Once again the objective genitive is verified, but the last sentence of this quote finds these Greek scholars mentioning "only the God-kind of faith" in direct reference to Mark 11:22. What does this mean? Does it mean God has His own kind of faith? No! Since God is clearly the object of faith in this verse, then "the kind of faith" Jesus is teaching is "the kind of faith" that is *fixed* on God, Who is our "object" of worship and praise. Such faith is found in Hebrews 11, enabling us to know and fulfill His will.

To ignore Hebrews 11 and build a faith doctrine on this one verse (Mark 11:22) without the translation support of the Greek in proper context is deceitful. Furthermore, if the apostles were convinced Jesus was teaching them and all who will follow Him to "Have the faith of God," why didn't they write it in some of the epistles as a reminder?

Also, did Jesus remind any of the seven churches He addressed and reproved in Revelation, chapters 2-3, to use their "faith of God" power to solve their problems and get into spiritual sync with Him? If Jesus had taught this "faith of God" principle while on the earth, then this would have been a crucial time to remind the churches and reestablish this "faith of God" doctrine. Then the believers could get right with God and their problems would be gone, and miracles would begin. But Jesus did not say a word about Mark 11:22. Follow what Jesus taught and you will avoid deception.

Despite the abundance of Greek evidence for contextual wisdom on Mark 11:22, there are those worldwide who still choose their own improper belief of Mark 11:22. In doing so, they seek to glorify their personal "faith picture" rather than honor His Name (Psalm 138:2).

Mark 11:23—You Can Have What You Say?

In his booklet, *You Can Have What You Say*, [20] Kenneth E. Hagin states Mark 11:23 teaches, "You can have what you say." This includes healing and money. Mark 11:23 is popular among Word of Faith believers, because for them, it portrays what some call miraculous mountain-moving faith. Let's look at this verse carefully to discern what the Lord Jesus wills for all of His followers to know. Does it assure that all who use this verse with unwavering faith are guaranteed to receive whatever they say?

> For verily I say unto you, That whosoever shall say to this mountain, Be thou removed, and be thou cast into the sea; and shall not doubt in his heart, but shall believe that those things which he saith shall come to pass; he shall have whatsoever he saith.

Is Jesus telling us that we can use this single verse to obtain health and wealth, or whatsoever we desire according to what we say? Is not what God says (His will) a priority over what we say (our will)?

To understand the context of Mark 11:23, we need to look back at verses 20-21. Peter commented that the fig tree Jesus had cursed was dried up and withered. The Lord Jesus responds by saying "Have faith in God" (verse 22), which leads to understanding verse 23. Jesus always knew His Father's will (John 4:34; 5:19-20; 6:38; 8:29) by spending substantial time in prayer (Luke 6:12; Hebrews 5:7-8). Therefore, the tree withering miracle paved the way for Jesus to teach about verse 23.

Jesus teaches them about "faith with the power to remove a mountain and cast it into the sea." He talks about not having doubt in your heart and believing what you say will come to pass. It is important to understand that in order for a mountain to move it would take a miracle, similar to what transpired in Exodus 14: 14-22. In this setting, the children of Israel thought Pharaoh had cornered them and death was coming. However, the LORD spoke to Moses saying, "But lift thou up thy rod, and stretch out thine hand over the sea, and divide it: and the children of Israel shall go on dry ground through the midst of the sea" (verse 16).

Moses did not doubt God and did as he was told. The miracle happened because it was God's will. Moses did not speak the miracle into existence with his own faith power. Rather it was God Who parted the sea with His miraculous power *after* Moses obeyed the LORD'S words of instruction. This example gives us a foundation for accepting and teaching God's definition of miraculous mountain-moving faith.

There is a miraculous *guideline* Jesus is teaching in this withering fig tree setting. When the LORD speaks to you and tells you to do something miraculous, He has ordained it, so do not doubt His words of instruction. Faith to believe for a miracle comes by hearing from God (Romans 10:17) in accordance with His will. We cannot just go around and speak, confess, decree, or declare a miracle of any kind unless God reveals to us that it is His will to do the miracle for us.

Speaking, confessing, or declaring one's will, as is common in false faith ministries, would be the sin of presumption (Psalm 19:13) and using the LORD'S Name in vain. The key to Mark 11:22-24 is to know the mind of God pertaining to the concern at hand, because God's will is involved in all of our prayers (1 John 5:14-15) and in all miracles (1 Corinthians 12:10-11).

In verse 24, Jesus continues His teaching with instructions on asking for things *in God's will* while praying, and believing you will receive them. Then Jesus switches the teaching from visible miracles (the fig tree) to invisible miracles becoming visible, by reminding us about the importance of forgiveness in verses 25-26. These verses also cause miraculous character changes that become visible when true forgiveness occurs.

Sometimes people have ongoing difficulty forgiving someone who has hurt them repeatedly or very deeply. They cry out to God, asking for help, begging for a spiritual miracle from Him to help them completely forgive the offender. When their request is granted, any grudge or ill will towards the offender is replaced by Christ's love and forgiveness. Such a character change is as obvious as a withered fig tree. Remember, Jesus and His Father are glorified from miracles that cause an inward spiritual transformation, or an outward physical change (healings, miracles of nature).

Too many people have taught *only* the first part of Mark 11:22-26 for the purpose of looking for physical miracles. They have overlooked what Jesus desired for us to know and apply about the miraculous spiritual healing availability also found in these verses. Forgiveness (inner healing) can bring amazing healing to all who are involved in the process, and improve our prayer life with our Father in heaven.

The Difference Between Presumption and Faith

Hebrews 11 gave numerous examples of faith that please God. The vast and obvious difference between faith that pleases God (verse 6) and presumption will now be shown. Psalm 19:13 is our teacher:

> Keep back thy servant also from presumptuous sins; let them not have dominion over me: then I shall be upright, and I shall be innocent from the great transgression.

The Psalmist wants God's help to keep him back from presumptuous sins, indicating the seriousness of this type of sin. This sin rules over its victims and establishes an ongoing dominion, one of constant control over any participant. It is so dominating that it is called "great" transgression (rebellion). Furthermore, the dominant sin of presumption was also punishable by death, as recorded in Deuteronomy 17:12-13; 18:20-22.

The word (*tolmētēs*) found in 2 Peter 2:10 describes people who are self-willed, daring, and presumptuous.[21] This is an accurate description of many who are involved with the Worldwide Faith Movement. They dare people to prove their faith by rejecting medicine and to claim their healing "By faith." They presume one is "already healed physically" through the shed blood of Jesus. Thus, they teach that "Strong and unwavering faith with a bold public confession will always cause God to heal you." This is not true, because Jesus and His apostles never taught this. It is sad, sinful, and disrespectful to the Lord Jesus that so many people are participants in "presumptuous false faith healing doctrine."

Another element contained within the sin of presumption needs to be emphasized. Presumption *breeds* a self-willed attitude, rather than an attitude of submission to God's will. This sin leads to constant rebellion against the LORD and has dominion over the sinner. Rebellion is the sin of witchcraft, and stubbornness (insubordination) is as iniquity and idolatry (1 Samuel 15:23).

When people choose a rebellious and presumptuous self-willed attitude, they could be opening *their* lives to demonic spirits to come into their presence and counterfeit the work of the Holy Spirit. In my experience helping people come out of the occult, former witches (Amy and Carly) told me they used demonic spirits to fulfill their desires or requests for what they wanted. As witches they *presumed* how the demons would respond to their declarations or affirmations of confident faith that came from using their witchcraft books. These former witches, who became Christians, had much success with their presumptuous methods for gain.

People embracing false faith teachings need to quit treating the LORD like He is a spiritual genie who responds to certain "faith-filled" words. Presumptuous false teaching about "faith-filled" words promotes the lordship of self and denies the Lordship of Jesus. Truly, "the just and righteous people of God shall live by faith," not by presumption (Hebrews 10:38).

Look back at the chapter title. Numerous false faith doctrines have been exposed. Anything false does not please God. Only by living in true faith can we be pleasing to the LORD. Hopefully, you are living in true faith. If not, repent as needed.

Endnotes:

1. W. E. Vine, *Vine's Expository Dictionary of New Testament Words* (Old Tappan, New Jersey: Fleming H. Revell, 1966), Vol. II. E – Li, p. 71.
2. James Strong, *Strong's Exhaustive Concordance of the Bible* (Nashville, Tennessee: Abingdon Press, 1976), p. 74.

3. Charles Capps, *Faith and Confession* (England, Arkansas: Capps Publishing, 1987), p. 25.

4. Ibid., p. 32.

5. Ibid., p. 79.

6. Ibid., p. 106.

7. Ibid., p. 113.

8. Ibid., p. 183.

9. Charles Capps, *The Tongue—A Creative Force* (England, Arkansas: Capps Publishing, 1987), p. 152.

10. Gloria Copeland, *God's Will is Prosperity* (Fort Worth, Texas: Kenneth Copeland Publications, 1978), p. 106.

11. Kenneth Copeland, *The Force of Faith* (Fort Worth, TX: Kenneth Copeland Publications, 1992), p. 10.

12. Ibid., p. 14.

13. Creflo A. Dollar Jr. *The Image of Righteousness You're More Than You Know* (Tulsa, Oklahoma: Harrison House, 2002), p. 43.

14. Don Gossett & E. W. Kenyon, *The Power of Your Words* (New Kensington, PA: Whitaker House, 1981), p. 132.

15. Kenneth E. Hagin, *Words* (Tulsa, OK: Kenneth Hagin Ministries, 1979), p. 29.

16. Andrew Wommack, *God Wants You Well* (Tulsa, OK: Harrison House, 2010), pp. 134, 135.

17. *Word Pictures in the New Testament,* Volume I, *The Gospels According to Matthew and Mark* (Nashville, TN: Broadman Press, 1930), p. 361.

18. R. C. H. Lenski, *The Interpretation of St. Mark's Gospel* (Minneapolis, Minnesota: Augsburg Publishing House, 1964), p. 493.

19. A. T. Robertson and W. Hersey Davis, *A New Short Grammar of the Greek Testament,* 10th ed. (Grand Rapids, Michigan: Baker Book House, 1982), pp. 227, 228.

20. Kenneth E. Hagin, *"You Can Have What You Say!"* (Tulsa, OK: Kenneth Hagin Ministries, 1979), p. 1.

21. W. E. Vine, *An Expository Dictionary of New Testament Words,* p. 267.

1 Timothy 6:9-11

But they that will be rich fall into temptation and a snare, and into many foolish and hurtful lusts, which drown men in destruction and perdition. For the love of money is the root of all evil: which while some coveted after, they have erred from the faith, and pierced themselves through with many sorrows. But thou, O man of God, flee these things; and follow after righteousness, godliness, faith, love, patience, meekness.

Chapter 10

Distorting Scriptures for Money

This chapter will reveal some deceitful ways "prosperity preachers" are presenting Bible verses to raise money. Prosperity ($) teachings from worldwide Word-Faith preachers will be compared to the Scriptures. Their *personal* interpretation of biblical prosperity verses will receive a contextual inspection to see if their "faith for money" doctrines are from the inspired Word of God, or their desired word of greed, due to misrepresenting prosperity verses (2 Peter 2:3; 3:16).

As you learn about various false teachings on biblical prosperity, keep in mind that Proverbs 19:22 says "The desire of a man is his kindness: and a poor man is better than a liar." Financially poor people who are *rich in truth* will go to heaven. Financially wealthy people who preach monetary distortion about God's Word will answer to the LORD of judgement (2 Corinthians 5:10; Revelation 21:8). Let's examine verses and teachings commonly taught among "prosperity teachers" who solicit love offerings because *they* love money.

What is Seed Faith?

In the last twenty years, there has been a significant increase in televangelists devoting more air time to preaching faith in financial prosperity rather than faith in the true Gospel. Many credit the late Oral Roberts (1918-2009) with laying the foundation of "seed faith" teaching about fifty years ago.[1] Financial "seed faith" planting is preached constantly worldwide. These false prosperity preachers proclaim that if you plant a "seed faith investment" in *their* ministry, God will bless you with a financial return if you have faith to receive it. Here's the problem; Jesus and His disciples never taught the Gospel was a financial system where money given to the work of the Gospel guaranteed your money back and even more, if you have faith.

However, they firmly say, "As a farmer sows a physical seed and expects a harvest by planting it in good soil and taking care of it, those of solid faith will sow a financial seed to their ministry." They assure you *their* ministry or their purpose for the money is the good seed soil. You must take care of your financial seed by keeping faith in your seed of obedient giving. If you don't get a return on your monetary investment, it is your fault due to wavering faith or doubt.

In 2 Corinthians 9:10, Paul says the seed sown (money) is multiplied for Gospel use, and it increases "the fruits of your righteousness." Paul does not say the "seed faith donation" will be money multiplied back to the givers *if* they have enough faith.

Still, some insist that if you plant a seed of financial faith in their ministry, "You can receive a 30, 60, or 100 fold financial blessing." They set up the unlearned listener by combining Mark 4:20 which states seed sown on good ground "brings forth *fruit,* some thirtyfold, some sixty, and some a hundred" with Mark 10:29-30.[2] These verses cite various blessings, including persecutions, but do not talk about exchanging faith for money. The seed is the Word of God (Luke 8:11). This false teaching makes the rich get richer, and the poor get poorer.

Is Luke 6:38 Money or Relationships?

Luke 6:38 is another verse that has been constantly distorted for decades by many in the world, even by those who are not Word of Faith preachers. It reads:

> Give and it shall be given unto you; good measure, pressed down, and shaken together, and running over, shall men give unto your bosom.

Gloria Copeland teaches that if the Mark 10:29-30 hundredfold ($) return, which was just refuted in the last section, "is too hard for you now, then when you give, act on Luke 6:38."[3] She writes:

Give, and [gifts] will be given to you; good measure, pressed down, shaken together, and running over, will they pour into [the pouch formed by] the bosom [of your robe and used as a bag]. For with the measure you deal out [with the measure you use when you confer benefits on others], it will be measured back to you. (Luke 6:38, *The Amplified Bible*). "This says what you give will be pressed down, shaken together, and running over. That is definitely a great increase. Sounds like a hundredfold return!"[4]

The Amplified version teaching on Luke 6:38 is definitely wrong. Whoever came up with this "personal amplified belief" did a terrible injustice to the words of the Word of God in the flesh! The bosom Jesus mentions is the heart of man, not a pouch for money or any material possession. When Jesus refers to "your bosom" in verse 38, He uses the Greek word *kŏlpŏs,* which is also used in Luke 16:22-23, John 1:18, and John 13:23. These verses have no connection with money, nor does verse 38 as we shall see.

To discern the exact context of Luke 6:38, we must look at verses 20-37 where Jesus begins His teaching in this section of Scripture. The Lord is instructing His followers about the proper attitude at all times, and adversity from those not in compliance with His words. Nowhere in verses 20-37 does Jesus teach that our Luke 6:38 reward is money. Our return for obedience to the words of Jesus is not financial gain, but prosperous relationships that produce abundant fruitful spiritual blessings (John 15:1-5; Galatians 5:22-23), and reward in heaven (verse 23). Notice in verse 24 the rich are not praised, but warned.

Can We Buy God's Protection? (Isaiah 54:17)

The beginning portion of Isaiah 54:17 says, "No weapon that is formed against thee shall prosper." During his *Breakthrough* program (TBN telecast on October 22, 2012), Pastor Rod Parsley of World

Harvest Church, Columbus, Ohio, talked about "a fierce battle raging against you and of everything of great value in your life." He went on to say: "On this broadcast you are about to discover for yourself how to receive His miraculous anointing of provision and protection."[5]

In an attempt to convince listeners to respond to Isaiah 54:17 by sowing monthly financial seed faith of $54.17 he says, "This is a moment of faith that may never, ever be repeated again." This last statement is a common fear factor "misled prosperity preachers" use to push people into giving money quickly to their ministry. This implies that if you don't give now, you will miss out on God's overall blessing and not have His protection. Giving is to be done in a cheerful manner (2 Corinthians 9:7), never forceful or out of fear, and not for the purpose of buying God's protection in all areas of our life.

Pastor Parsley is wrong in teaching people they can use Isaiah 54:17 as a verse to buy protection from "a fierce battle raging against you and of everything of great value in your life." If his teaching on Isaiah 54:17 were true, then why pray for your family, finances, marriage, or health? Just donate monthly, which buys and guarantees God's protection. Relax, and forget about John 14:13 and Philippians 4:6-8.

There is no proof the LORD spoke to Pastor Parsley and told him to proclaim Isaiah 54:17 for money. What is the warranty on Isaiah 54:17? Is it a monthly or an annual renewal, and what happens if at some time in your life you no longer give according to Isaiah 54:17? Do you lose God's provisions and protection, and come under a curse? This is terrible distortion of a verse for money. Jesus did not use Scripture to squeeze money out of anyone who heard His messages.

Money is not mentioned in Isaiah 54:17. This verse is not about giving money to anyone for a miraculous anointing, protection, and provision. You can't buy God's power or bribe Him for protection and provision with money. Simon the sorcerer learned this (Acts 8:9-23). Our Lord's instructive protection to resist demonic attacks or any weapon that will ever come against us is given *freely* in Ephesians 6:10-18, and it works!

Does 3 John 2 Promise Wealth?

Globally, false prosperity preachers insist 3 John 2 is God's will for all to prosper financially. John writes *directly* to Gaius (verse 1), *not* all Christians. The *King James Bible* is commonly used in Word of Faith congregations. They should remember that when "thou" is used, as in 3 John 2 in reference to Gaius, it is in the Greek singular, not the plural. John wrote this verse to Gaius *only*. This means any who teach 3 John 2 is God's will for all Christians to be financially prosperous and healed are wrong.

Dr. Floyd Nolen Jones explains the singular/plural use in his book *Which Version is The Bible?* [6] The following authors mislead people by teaching 3 John 2 assures wealth and/or health for *all* Christians:

Rod Parsley—*Your Harvest Is Come*, 1999, p. 26.
Benny Hinn—*"Rise & Be Healed!"* 1991, p. 66.
Gloria Copeland—*God's Will is Prosperity*, 1978, p. 45.
Guillermo Maldonado—*Jesus Heals Your Sickness Today*, 2009, p. 28.
Andrew Wommack—*God Wants You Well*, 2010, pp. 38, 127.
Joseph Prince—*Healing Promises*, 2012, p. 61.
Charles Capps—*The Tongue–A Creative Force*, 1995, p. 66.
Joyce Meyer—*Prepare to Prosper*, 1997, p. 46.
Oral Roberts—*Miracle of Seed-Faith*, 1970, p. 87.
Creflo Dollar Jr—*The Image of Righteousness You're More Than You Know*, 2002, pp. 173-174.
E. W. Kenyon & Don Gossett—*Speak Life*, 2013, p. 172.

The list of people just cited is a small representation of various authors around the world who do not teach the proper context of 3 John 2. John's wish/desire for God to continue blessing Gaius was because of his "charity before the church," and helping those who went forth for the Name of Jesus (3 John 5-8).

Did Jesus Leave Heaven to Make Us Rich?

Prosperity preachers often cite 2 Corinthians 8:9 for proof that God's will is financial riches for all Christians. Kenneth Copeland writes that "Jesus came to minster to the poor.... The Bible said He became poor that we might become rich (2 Corinthians 8:9). He bore the curse of poverty in order to get us out of it, not to leave us in it."[7] This verse reads:

> For ye know the grace of our Lord Jesus Christ, that, though He was rich, yet for your sakes He became poor, that ye through His poverty might become rich.

Notice the word "grace" in this verse. It's not "grace for money." The context of this verse is *not* about financial prosperity for all. It's about spiritual prosperity in our relationship with the Lord Jesus. Paul does not lead into this verse by mentioning money in the previous verse, and does not mention money in the verse after. The Son of God left the riches of heaven where everything was perfect to enter our imperfect world of fallen sinners and become the propitiation for our sins (1 John 2:2). When this was accomplished, all who repented and received Him as Lord and Savior would become spiritually rich with forgiveness and obtain a future eternal heavenly reward.

Paul would not want anyone who ever reads 2 Corinthians 8:9 to think he is emphasizing that financial prosperity for all is God's will, because he wrote in Galatians 2:10 he was aware of poverty in the Body of Christ. Also, Paul did not say Jesus "bore the curse of poverty in order to get us out of it" when recording 2 Corinthians 8:9.

Even Jesus knew of poverty in the Church at Smyrna (Revelation 2:9), and didn't tell them to remember He came from heaven "to bear the curse of poverty" to make Christians rich. Historically, the early Messianic Jews and Christians were not known for their abundance of money throughout the Roman Empire. As ambassadors for Christ (2 Corinthians 5:20), they were known for their abundant life (John 10:10), which was focused on the spiritual riches of grace that Jesus had freely given them. Ambassadors for Christ always emphasize His spiritual riches, daily grace, and mercy (Lamentations 3:22-25).

Miracles From Proverbs 18:21?

This verse is often spoken and "confessed" among Word of Faith advocates because some believe the tongue, when used with faith-filled words, is filled with the power to change circumstances in their life (health and wealth) in a miraculous way. But does Proverbs 18:21 lay a foundation for miraculous health and wealth, or is it a guideline for wisely selected words that bear spiritual fruit? It reads:

> Death and life are in the power of the tongue: and they that love
> it shall eat the fruit thereof.

If we look at the verses before and after verse 21, we can discern that they don't cite anything on health and wealth. Therefore, to use Proverbs 18:21 to speak miraculous health and/or wealth into your life is adding to God's Word, and He warns us not to do this in Proverbs 30:5-6. Proverbs 18:21 is Scriptural advice for guarding our speech so we don't offend God and man, for we will eat the verbal fruit thereof.

From experience, we all know we wish we could take back certain words we have spoken during our lifetime, words that brought anguish and an unpleasant end (spiritual death) to a discussion. And there have been other times when our words were seasoned with edification (Ephesians 4:29-30; 1 Peter 4:11) and brought hope, faith, love, and encouragement (spiritual life) to all who were present. Follow the LORD'S guideline in these verses, and you will see how appropriate words will bear reciprocal spiritual fruit for the glory of our risen Savior.

The Blessing of Abraham's Covenant

Concerning Abraham's Covenant from God, Gloria Copeland writes, "When the Church received spiritual redemption, she let go of the rest of the blessing of Abraham. Prosperity and healing became a lost reality. The Church took spiritual blessing and left the prosperity and healing portions of the promise."[8] This doctrine is incorrect. A careful reading of chapters 12-17 in Genesis will reveal Abraham's Covenant was about his seed, land rights, and circumcision. Though Abraham was wealthy, nowhere in these chapters is physical healing and wealth promised to all future New Covenant believers.

Luke 1:67-79 mentions Abraham's Covenant. Health and wealth are not recorded. Romans 4:1-5:2 cites multiple references about Abraham's blessing, but does not teach this covenant provides health and wealth for all New Covenant believers. Galatians 3:8 explains God's plan to justify the heathen through faith. Verse 13 cites being redeemed from the curse (our sins) of the Law, not poverty/sickness redemption. Verse 14 reveals Abraham's blessing for the Gentiles; they would "receive the promise of the Spirit through faith." The apostle Paul was Holy Spirit-inspired to write Romans and Galatians, and records Abraham's "Covenant blessing" provides forgiveness (justification), not money, and certainly not physical healing.

False Faith Tithing Teachings

Malachi 3:7-12 records God's Old Covenant discussion with His Jewish people concerning tithing. God rebukes them because they have robbed Him by not honoring Him with tithes and offerings and says, "Ye are cursed with a curse: for ye have robbed Me, even this whole nation" (verse 9). A "false prosperity preacher" teaches this about Malachi 3:7-12:

Malachi 3:8 says you are robbing God if you don't tithe 10% of your earnings. And verse 9 says you are cursed with a curse because you have robbed and stolen from God by not tithing. Verse 10 says God will not pour out a blessing to you from heaven until you give your tithe. Release the money in your hand to God, and God will release the money in His hand to you. Get out your checkbook now and break the curse by sending your tithe to this ministry, and God will rebuke the devourer of your finances.

This preacher was emphatically talking about tithing money and financial offerings, not a tithing and offering of "food" or the fruits of the ground as recorded in verses 10-12. Verse 11 says the devourer is rebuked from destroying the fruits of the ground, not your finances. Verse 12 says "And all the nations shall call you blessed: for ye shall be a delightsome land." The phrase "open the windows of heaven" does not refer to God sending money from the sky to their yards or fields for pick up. The rain and sun will prosper their crops.

The Malachi 3 quote is a false prosperity teaching. Proponents twist the Scriptures to make you think God wants to prosper you, and they use fear tactics to extort money out of the deceived. Jesus and His disciples never used this "tithing fear tactic" for money. They were supported by devoted and thankful followers (Luke 8:1-3).

Another false teaching on tithing from Malachi 3:7-12 says tithing covers two financial areas:

Since you have robbed God by not tithing, you must begin tithing. In addition to the tithe, you must also give a money offering to break the curse of the devourer, or Satan will continue to devour your finances.

People who begin tithing do not have to give a tithe, *and* an additional financial offering to please God and control the devil.

Are Word of Faith Televangelists Misleading Millions?

Have the faith preachers, who teach falsely on tithing when using Malachi 3:7-12, stopped to realize that they might be *opening* up the gates of Hades for curses of deception, rather than the windows of heaven? And have they considered that *their* Scriptural distortion offends God? Beware of all ministries that tell you how financially blessed you will be "if" you give to *their* ministry.

A final concern must be addressed. There are false faith preaching ministries that help the poor and needy in various parts of the world. Though they are doing good deeds in areas of need, this question needs an answer: Are the people they are helping being taught false doctrine about Jesus and what His shed blood represents? If so, they are purposely offending "little ones" by causing them to stumble in true belief about Jesus. Mixing false doctrine with food and clothing does not please the Lord Jesus (Matthew 18:6).

The next chapter will furnish insight on how they believe they can send angels on monetary assignments. Did Jesus do this?

Endnotes:

1. Oral Roberts, *Miracle of Seed-Faith* (no city or state given: Fleming H. Revell Publishing, 1970).
2. Gloria Copeland, *God's Will is Prosperity* (Fort worth, TX: Kenneth Copeland Publications, 1978), pp. 70-71.
3. Ibid., p. 87.
4. Ibid., p. 87.
5. Justin Peters, *Clouds Without Water* (DVD), (Edmond, Oklahoma: Justin Peters Productions, 2013), disc 2.
6. Floyd Nolen Jones, *Which Version is The Bible?* (Humboldt, Tennessee: Kings Word Press, 2014), pp. 78-79.
7. Kenneth Copeland, *Prosperity: The Choice is Yours* (Fort Worth, Texas: Kenneth Copeland Publications, 1994), p. 26.
8. Gloria Copeland, *God's Will is Prosperity*, p. 25.

Chapter 11

Holy Angels or Prosperity Deception?

Angels are a common Word of Faith topic. Many believe we can use Hebrews 1:14 to command the angels around us to get money for needs and ministry. This verse says angels are "sent forth [by God] to minister." For many years, "faith and confession" ministers have taught that Christians can assign God's holy angels specific duties of ministry. They believe the angels are waiting to hear what your words of faith will direct them to do.

The best way to educate you on this worldwide belief concerning angels for ministry would be to list several quotes. Then you will be aware of their doctrines of angels on assignment.

Charles Capps: *Faith and Confession*
> *Confessing God's Word works for you because it puts the angels to work for you* (page 213).

> **Truth:** According to Scripture, angels respond to God's spoken Word and "do His commandments" for ministry (Psalm 103:20-21). No verse says we can use the written Word to "put the angels to work" as we desire.

Charles Capps and Annette Capps: *Angels*
> We have the ability as people born of God to summon the aid of angels. This is a part of our salvation (page 63).

> **Truth:** If you check all the verses Jesus and the apostles taught about our salvation, you won't find one that says summoning the aid of angels "is a part of our salvation."

> **Capps:** The ministry of angels is available to you.... The angels will get involved in your finances, your business affairs, and your family affairs (pages 66, 67).

Truth: Paul never told the various congregations he started that "the ministry of angels" was available to help in money, business, and family affairs. Isn't the Holy Spirit Who dwells within us (Romans 8:9, 11) going to help us for a lifetime (John 14:16-17) according to God's will?

Capps: As you speak God's Word in faith with your own mouth, you commission the angels to move according to that Word.... *You* have legal authority to call upon these ministering spirits to work in your behalf (pages 89, 90).

Truth: There is no place found in Scripture that says we have "legal authority to call upon" angels to work for us. Speaking Bible verses out loud does not cause angels to minister for us.

Capps: The angels are waiting for you to say things that will loose them! Begin to speak the Word of God. **Loose your angels!** (pages 94, 95, bold in original).

Truth: Repeatedly, the Capps family teaches things about angels not found in the Bible. Jesus never taught the apostles to loose their angels by speaking Scripture out loud.

Capps: The power of binding and loosing is held by the believer here on earth. That power operates through words. You can bind your angels by just a few words of unbelief! (pages 117, 118).

Truth: No Scripture teaches believers have "the power" to bind or loose *God's* holy angels by what they say. They are His angels for ministry, not ours! (Psalm 103:20-21).

Gloria Copeland: *God's Will is Prosperity*

In the name of Jesus, I take authority over the money I need.... I command you to come to me.... Ministering spirits, you go and cause it to come (page 63).

Truth: Did Jesus remind His followers in Revelation 2:9 they could command their angels to go out to obtain money, thereby removing their poverty? To have the opportunity to help those in need is an opportunity to show our love for them, which glorifies our Lord Jesus.

Mrs. Copeland: The angels are in the earth to prosper you (page 117).
Truth: As usual, no verse support for this belief because there isn't any. Hebrews 1:14 does not say angels are ministering "spirits of money."

Mrs. Copeland: Your words put the angels to work on your behalf to bring to pass whatever you say.... The angels are waiting on your words (page 121).
Truth: Our gracious God (Hebrews 4:15-16) waits upon our words. We are taught in the Old Covenant and New Covenant to pray, seek, call upon, and request from the LORD, not to use our words to send out any angels.

Kenneth Copeland: *The Laws of Prosperity*
The Bible also says that angels hearken to the Word of God (see Psalm 103:20), so when you use the Word in the Name of Jesus, they are obligated to follow your command (page 102).
Truth: Yes, angels hearken to the word that God tells them to do (His voice of instruction), not our voice of instruction. To believe that using the Name of Jesus makes angels "obligated to follow your command" sounds like taking authority over them. In 1 Peter 3:22, we find that "angels and authorities" are subject to Jesus. His voice tells them how to minister to us.

All of these quotes just refuted about angels on assignment for gathering money, or doing something for you, are not backed by one Scripture of truth. They have been conceived by rejecting what Psalm 103:20-21 and 1 Peter 3:22 clearly teach about the ministry of angels. Angelic ministry is the Lord's assignment, not ours.

The great apostle Paul knew Jesus well (Galatians 1:11-12), and spent time with the apostles (Acts 15:1-2). He went through numerous hardships (1 Corinthians 4:11-16; 2 Corinthians 4:8-10; 11:23-27; Philippians 4:12). If Jesus didn't instruct Paul to use angels as a remedy for any of these problems, then we can be sure that *His words* (1 Peter 3:22) control the angels mentioned in Hebrews 1:14.

Even the late Kenneth E. Hagin (1917-2003) was convinced angels are for gathering money. He declared that Jesus personally spoke to him[5] and said the following:

> Claim whatever you need or want. Say, "Satan, take your hands off my finances." Then say, "Go, ministering spirits, and cause the money to come."[6]

This couldn't have been the real Jesus who spoke to Mr. Hagin, because the real Jesus knows the context of Hebrews 1:14, and Jesus also knows angels are subject to Him *only* (1 Peter 3:22). Acts 5:17-20 and 27:23-24 provide more evidence that Christ's chosen apostles didn't have permission to direct angels, or have authority for sending angels to gather money for them. And Jesus didn't tell angels to get Him money during His ministry. Christians have been given authority to cast out demons, *as guided by the Holy Spirit,* but they have not been given authority to send out God's holy angels for any purpose.

In conclusion, the ministering spirits of false angelic teachings sound more like occult prosperity spirits than holy angels. Stay away from this unbiblical doctrine. Let the Lord Jesus send *His* angels.

Anointed Prayer Items They Sell for Healing

For decades faith teachers have been sending out items such as olive oil or water in small vials or bottles, and healing cloths. They claim these items are "anointed by God" through their prayers. When you donate to *their* ministry, they will send you one of these items as a reminder to increase your faith to receive healing or deliverance from evil. These faith healing ministers and "prosperity preachers" say the apostle Paul healed this way in Acts 19:11-12 which reads:

> And God wrought special miracles by the hands of Paul: So that from his body were brought unto the sick handkerchiefs or aprons, and the diseases departed from them, and the evil spirits went out of them.

Verse 11 records this was a time of special miracles, not a regular miraculous time that always occurred during Paul's ministry or the many other apostolic travels. Sometimes "prosperity preachers" use these verses when they are struggling financially. They say the olive oil is from Israel, the water is blessed and holy, and the prayer cloths have a special healing or miracle anointing for any part of your body needing healing. Also, they assure you they will pray over the items to be sent out. Just send them the amount of money they are suggesting and your special miracle items will be shipped to you.

Questions to consider: Does the oil or water work until the vial is empty? How many times will the prayer cloth do a healing or cast out a demon? What happens if you wash it? Is the anointing gone? Can you reorder for more miracles? I am not being sarcastic. This is a scam and people continue to fall for it.

Sometimes they say these items are a "contact point" enabling you to connect with the power of the LORD. However, Bible prayer verses don't mention "physical contact points" being *needed* when praying to the LORD for healing, financial help, or casting out demons. Our faith should be focused on the LORD, not on any material object. If our faith is in "physical objects" as contact points for help, we are in contact with sin.

In the occult, physical objects (crystals, amulets, charms) are used as "contact points" to attract demons for a specific purpose. As Christians in need, we pray to God Who is the object of our faith, and never use physical objects as a spiritual focus "to activate" miraculous power. Healing from objects is not Holy Spirit healing.

Any person who offers *any object* for sale claiming it will do Holy Spirit miracles is not ministering in the Name of the real Jesus. If you have any physical objects you have paid for to increase your faith to receive what you are seeking (healing or money), destroy them (Deuteronomy 7:26; Acts 19:18-20). True faith comes by hearing and hearing by the Word of God (Romans 10:17), so focus on the LORD for all your needs. False faith for healing or money comes by placing faith in a physical object.

A deceptive way these ministers get people to send money to them is to say something such as, "We will send you the healing cloth for free. Just call us and we will ship it to you. And when you call, remember to sow your financial seed faith of any amount to this ministry." Suddenly, the healing cloth/demon removing cloth has money attached to it. Though they say you get the cloth for free, they are manipulating you to send *them* money. This is not of the LORD.

Jesus and His disciples didn't heal and cast out demons for money (Matthew 10:5-10). Also, Paul did not charge for the miracles the LORD did with the aprons and cloths in Acts 19:11-12, nor did he tell *the grace recipients* their "prayer-cloth faith" determined if they received a miracle. The LORD performs healings, casts out demons, and manifests miracles for free, according to His grace. God does not have a biblical health, wealth, and deliverance menu that allows people to order by request, and then charges money for purchasing His miraculous service.

Is it possible that healing cloths are contact points, sometimes accompanied by demonic spirits to fulfill people's desires, thereby bringing more attached deception into their lives? Satan copied the miracles done through Moses (Exodus 7:9-12; 8:5-7). Demonic healing spirits are common in the occult. They can counterfeit the work of the Holy Spirit (Deuteronomy 13:1-4). If you are a Christian, just make contact with Jesus through prayer and forget about using any physical object for receiving healing or provision for any need.

Another unbiblical method used to convince people to donate money is to tell them that *their* books, music, and DVDs they are offering "are anointed by God." They say your house will be anointed if you have these items. One television preacher said the music CD he was offering for sale would make your home "a demon-free home." Did Jesus teach this "use of objects" method to eliminate demons? Is this demon-home-cleansing "use of objects" taught by Paul in Ephesians 6:10-18? An important purpose for God's anointing is to keep us from being deceived (1 John 2:20, 27). Don't be deceived. Don't donate to false prosperity teachings.

Shofars and Tallits

There is also a false prosperity teaching on the shofar. The shofar is a ram's horn blown for certain religious Jewish festivals and on certain days. One television minister, who was selling this horn, said if you blew it around your house or outside you would drive all demons away. There were shofars during the time of Jesus, and He didn't teach this, nor did His apostles. Jesus didn't "blow out" demons with His personal shofar. He cast them out (Mark 1:23-39), as did His disciples (Matthew 10:1; Luke 10:17-20; Acts 16:16-18). Biblical guidelines for standing firm against the devil are given in Ephesians 6:10-18 and James 4:7.

The Tallit, the Jewish prayer shawl, is another item that has been marketed more in recent years. Some "prosperity retailers" say this prayer shawl is so protective that when you pray, "Just cover your head and shoulders with it, and no demonic darts (bad thoughts from Satan) can penetrate the Tallit." If this were true, why didn't Paul tell us about the Tallit in Ephesians 6:10-18 when he carefully explained the armor of God? Selling the Tallit for protection is unbiblical and fosters deception.

Corrupting the Lord's Prayer

False "prosperity preachers" also teach that the words "Thy kingdom come, Thy will be done on earth as it is in heaven" (Matthew 6:10) mean: "Since there is no poverty in heaven, God's will is no poverty on earth among Christians." When Jesus taught this prayer, He did not say anything about money. His teaching covered acknowledging God's Holiness, food, forgiveness, temptation, and deliverance from evil. This prayer is for God's daily will and direction within our lives. If wealth is implied in The Lord's Prayer, it is spiritual wealth which improves our relationship with Jesus.

Beware of "fundraising prophets and preachers" who find a verse, and say something like this: "The LORD spoke to me and said Psalm 70:1. He wants 70 people to donate $70 a month for one year to this ministry so He can prosper and protect you." Using Scriptures like this sounds more like occult Numerology than trusting the LORD to provide (Proverbs 3:5-6).

The "kingdom of false prosperity teachings" is worldwide. Enormous repentance is needed from *all* false prosperity teachers *and* their followers. They need to repent of all false doctrine for money. Then they need to preach true biblical prosperity as Jesus taught it, proving they are repentant.

Endnotes:

1. Charles Capps, *Faith and Confession* (England, AR: Capps Publishing, 1987).
2. Charles and Annette Capps, *Angels* (England, Arkansas: Capps Publishing, 1984).
3. Gloria Copeland, *God's Will is Prosperity* (Fort Worth, Texas: Kenneth Copeland Publications, 1978).
4. Kenneth Copeland, *The Laws of Prosperity* (Fort Worth, Texas: Kenneth Copeland Publications, 1974).
5. Kenneth E. Hagin, *How God Taught Me About Prosperity* (Tulsa, Oklahoma: Rhema Bible Church, 1985), p. 23.
6. Ibid., p. 18.

Chapter 12

They Said it: Is it True?

Quotes in this chapter will strongly confirm that various false faith doctrines and beliefs are not even close to lining up with Scripture. You will see how they add to Scripture (Proverbs 30:5-6), proving they are unlearned and wrest the Scripture to their desire (2 Peter 3:16). Prepare for a long chapter with some strange, unsound, and bizarre beliefs from men and women who misrepresent Scripture.

Gloria Copeland: *God's Will is Prosperity*

Your words control your destiny. Your life right now is the product of your words (page 122).

Truth: The Bible does not teach that our words control our destiny, and that your life "is the product of your words." This belief totally pushes God away for His destiny in our life. Choosing our path with our words sounds exactly like what we did *before* we gave our lives to Jesus. We recognize Him as Lord by the way we allow Him to control our destiny. The LORD has more control of our destiny and our life than we sometimes realize (Deuteronomy 32:39; Ephesians 3:20).

Kenneth Copeland: *The Laws of Prosperity*

It is the force of faith which makes the laws of the spirit world function (page 15).

Truth: Two things are incorrect with this teaching: 1) There is no Bible verse which defines faith as a force. 2) The phrase, "laws of the spirit world," is never connected to any biblical faith teaching, and is not found in Scripture. The Holy Spirit did not set up "laws of the spirit world" where He functions by *our* force of faith. The substance of our faith (Hebrews 11:1) is obedience to God's will, and does not cause the Holy Spirit to submit to what we say.

Creflo Dollar: *The Image of Righteousness*

Yet this question kept coming to my mind: *Why would Jesus give me all authority in heaven and earth if I were not supposed to exercise it?* (page 101).

Truth: This question that kept coming to Mr. Dollar's mind was not from the Holy Spirit because Jesus said, "All power is given unto Me in heaven and in earth" (Matthew 28:19). No Christian has ever been given *all* authority in heaven and earth.

Jesse Duplantis: *Heaven—Close Encounters of the God Kind*

I had my first encounter of the God kind when I was about nine years old.... After I got into bed, I experienced something like a dream, yet it wasn't a dream. It was more like a vision. There was thunder and lightning; then I saw the face of a man with a grey beard coming toward me in the sky. He started hollering at me, saying, "Fear God boy! Fear God!" (page 20). He also says, "I was aware of His Spirit around me at all times. I could feel and sense the presence of God" (page 21).

Truth: How would Jesse, as a young, unsaved boy, be sure this was God's presence? Is there a biblical example of this?

Duplantis: I can remember walking down school halls feeling God's presence around me (page 22). When he was 17 years old, his mother had this dream about Jesse: "She said I was standing on a beach with a tidal wave of the blood of Jesus flowing over me" (page 23).

Truth: What biblical proof verifies this dream of tidal wave blood was from Jesus? Anyone can have strange dreams.

Duplantis: As I grew older, I couldn't seem to go anywhere without feeling God's presence. But I still got more into sin (page 28). Jesse describes a night when God came into his bedroom as a wind "so strong in fact that the curtains started flying up over the rods." An audible voice said to Jesse, "You asked to see Me; turn around" (page 39).

They Said it: Is it True?

Truth: Other than the wind and a voice, which the devil can counterfeit, nothing significant happened. Is there any biblical fruit in this spiritual encounter?

Duplantis: I looked up and saw at the foot of my bed the biggest character I had ever seen in my life.... He just stood there looking at me. It was an angel of the Lord!... He said, "I have been sent by the Lord. You are under much stress, and the Lord sent me to tell you to sleep" (page 52).
Truth: With all the troubles and difficult times Paul records in 1 Corinthians 4:10-13, the Lord Jesus never sent angels to tell them to sleep, and they needed it much more than comfortable American Christians.

Duplantis: I have had many angels come when I have been preaching (page 53).... There were maybe a hundred people there at the service. As I was preaching, I turned toward the seats where the choir usually sits and saw that those seats were filled with angels! They looked like shafts of light.... One of them walked right by me and smiled at me.... As they walked down through the church, everybody just fell to the floor under the power of God. *Boom!* I was the only person left standing. About thirty minutes later, people began to get up off the floor and sit back down in the pews (page 54).
Truth: Nowhere in the Bible is it taught that the Lord Jesus sends holy angels to slay His people in the spirit; and in the middle of preaching the Word? To think that some misled people believe doing *nothing* for thirty minutes on the floor glorifies God (Ephesians 5:15-17) shows deep deception.

Duplantis: I heard a sound, *Whoosh!* And I was pulled up out of the room!... I don't know whether I was in my body or out of my body. He then describes zooming along "in something like a cable car" or a "chariot without a horse" (page 69). Upon arriving in heaven, he says he saw thousands of people lined up alongside the River of Life as it flowed throughout Paradise. "They had all been brought there in those chariot-like vehicles, the same as I was" (page 71).

Truth: When Paul writes about us meeting the Lord in the sky (1 Corinthians 15:51-55; 1 Thessalonians 4:16-18), he does not mention us being taken up in chariots. And no cable car or chariot took him up in 2 Corinthians 12:1-4.

Duplantis: Then I saw God's finger barely move and when it moved, an angel that was flying near Him was thrown up against a wall. *Bam!* It didn't hurt the angel (page 115).

Truth: According to his observation, God threw His angel against a wall. That doesn't sound like a heavenly Paradise. Is there any verse that teaches the LORD abuses His ministering spirits in heaven?

Duplantis: Jesus preached of His coming to earth.... As He preached, people—even though they were in new celestial bodies—fell under the power of God. Even in heavenly bodies they fell under God's power! (pages 116, 117).

Truth: When Jesus preached on the earth during His ministry with a great anointing, He did *not* slay anyone in the spirit. There is no Scriptural reason for Him to preach in heaven and knock people down with God's power.

Duplantis: Jesse says he talked with the apostle Paul in heaven and Paul reminded him, "It isn't them that liveth, but Christ that liveth in them" (page 159).

Truth: Paul didn't speak the King James dialect on earth so why would he speak it in heaven? This book that talks about a trip to heaven does not line up with Scripture.

Over the years, I have heard more and more people featured on Christian television saying they have been to heaven. They talk about what they saw and heard. Before they share a few minutes on their trip to heaven, it becomes very clear that their heavenly visit reveals things that are not found in the Bible about heaven. Examples are: rooms with body parts for healing not claimed, extra books for more biblical understanding, new ways to have heavenly visitations, a healing ministry given from Jesus while in heaven, and a new translation of Scripture. Such fraudulent heavenly visits qualify as delusional or demonic spiritual cinemas. The Bible gives sufficient descriptions of our future eternal home in 2 Corinthians 12:1-4 and Revelation 21-22.

John Hagee: *The Power to Heal*

Miracles happen every day to those who know how to release the power of God through faith, according to his word (page 7).
Truth: The key to miracles is not releasing "the power of God through faith," but His will (1 Corinthians 12:10-11). On pages 8-10, pastor Hagee details his mother's "miraculous healing" from colon cancer. The cancer was surgically removed and his mother recovered. Such a healing does not qualify as a miracle. It was medical intervention supported by prayer. True miracles override the physical laws of nature *instantly*. Examples are instant miraculous healings (John 5:5-9), changing water to wine (John 2:1-11), calming a storm (Luke 8:22-25), and multiplying fish and bread (Luke 9:12-17). Doesn't Mr. Hagee know the difference between a miracle and doctors providing medical help? (Colossians 4:14). This false teaching about healing miracles is also found in other "faith ministries."

Hagee: Let's look first at *how* Jesus healed. In Matthew 8:16 Jesus healed en masse. He was talking to a massive congregation and when he pronounced a healing prayer, they began to get well all over the building (page 41).
Truth: Matthew 8:16 reads: "When the even was come, they brought Him many that were possessed with devils: and He cast out the spirits with His word, and healed all that were sick." This verse doesn't say anything about Jesus being in a massive

congregation and pronouncing a healing prayer "all over the building." It records demonic deliverance and healings taking place at separate times. Why did pastor Hagee falsify this very clear Scriptural information? It's more common among Word-Faith ministers than most people realize, and adding to God's Word is becoming more acceptable among the deceived.

John Hagee: *The Power of the Prophetic Blessing*

Love is not what you say; love is what you *do*! (page 249).

As believers, we must touch in order to bless (page 251).

Truth: Has Mr. Hagee read 1 Corinthians 13? Love is *both* what you say and what you do! Also, *both* touch and words can be a blessing (Luke 24:53; Hebrews 6:14; James 3:9-10). When done gently and with edification (Romans 14:19), both touch and words are a blessing.

Kenneth Hagin: *How You Can Be Led By the Spirit of God*

Paul calls man's spirit "the inward man." Peter calls man's spirit "the hidden man of the heart" (page 6). My spirit will not tell me something wrong. It has the nature of God in it.... Whatever your spirit tells you will be right (page 99).

Truth: This teaching accentuates why it is difficult to get Word of Faith followers to admit they are deceived by false doctrine. They are convinced that when they are born-again, their spirit has the nature of God *in* it, and to them, this means they have the truth. So when you have a disagreement with them they might say, "My spirit does not bear witness to that." They totally ignore the fact that our inward man (man's spirit) is not perfect, and is going through daily renewal (2 Corinthians 4:16). Also, a Christian can have a seared conscience resulting from demonic doctrinal deception (1 Timothy 4:1), which can block truth. And the false Worldwide Faith Movement has multitudes of false doctrines quite capable of searing any receptive conscience. To believe your human spirit has God's nature in it is one of the ways they try to reinforce the belief that Christians become "gods" when they are born-again. This teaching is occult New Age belief, because it directs the user to "Look within Thyself" for guidance, rather than always allowing the Bible to correct and ground in truth as needed. Such a mindset establishes a spiritual foundation for resisting Scriptural reproof and correction as needed, which goes against the Word of God (Acts 17:11; 2 Timothy 2:15; 3:16-17). Furthermore, Romans 8:9 confirms that God's Spirit dwells in man, *not in* man's spirit. If God's spiritual nature was "in" man's spirit, this co-mingling of two natures would make both God and man hybrids, which the Bible does not teach.

Marilyn Hickey: *Your Pathway to Miracles*

In reference to Mark 11:23, she says, "Mountains must have ears. In other words, they respond when we speak to them in faith" (page 159).

Truth: Did Jesus say that mountains have ears? Her belief adds to the Lord's words, and makes her sound like there is a New Age Mystical consciousness in the physical mountain matter. Will Word-Faith people ever accept that their words don't create or cause miracles? It is the power and will of God (1 Corinthians 12:10-11). Defying the verses in the last sentence, she insists that miracles start with "I can," not "I can't" (page 98). Such a teaching totally puts man in control of miracles and rejects the Almighty will of God.

Mrs. Hickey: That night, before I went out to preach, I prayed, "Lord, You better show up and show off. This is Your name on the line, not my name" (page 107).

Truth: Here is tragic example of a faith person telling the Almighty that He "better show up and show off." This is not prayer, but telling the LORD what to do. Who is Lord? Did Jesus ever portray Himself as a spiritual "showoff," or display such a demanding attitude in prayer? (Hebrews 5:7).

Mrs. Hickey: The following occurred while Mrs. Hickey was speaking at a church in New Jersey. She saw a man in the back of the auditorium who was sitting in a wheelchair. She could see the man from only the waist up, and told him, "In Jesus' name, get up and walk." Well, he didn't get up and walk. So, I got very loud and "anointed," and I said, "In Jesus' name, get up and walk." But he still did not get up and walk.... David, an assistant pastor beside the man said, "Marilyn, he doesn't have any legs" (page 90).

Truth: Well, there's not much to say, except she was *not* "anointed" for healing that night, and did not hear from the Lord to tell the man to get up. Either she heard from her deceived mind, or an evil spirit seduced her to abuse the Name of Jesus. What is really sad about this situation is that similarities have occurred in other so-called miracle healing ministries. Years ago, a friend of mine watched a faith healing minister command people in wheelchairs to get up and walk. None of them did, but some slipped out of their wheelchair to the floor and began trying to move and slither. None were healed. The healer said to them: "You must build your faith more before you can receive your healing." Jesus and the apostles healed instantly, and they never sent people away telling them to increase their faith to be healed. Mrs. Hickey says she has read the Bible "fifty-five times" (page 225). How many more times will she need to read it before she honors the Name of Jesus concerning the gifts of healing?

Benny Hinn: *Welcome Holy Spirit*

The moment I said "Holy Spirit," He would come. My room would fill up with an atmosphere so electric and so beautiful that my entire body would begin to tingle. And as that presence would intensify, a numbness would come on me (page 44).

Truth: So, all Benny Hinn has to say is "Holy Spirit" and God, the Holy Spirit, comes to him? Did Jesus teach anything like this in prayer, or when He described the functions of the Holy

Spirit in John 14-16? Please read these chapters, and build a proper understanding of Who dwells in you (Romans 8:9, 11). And where do we find in Scripture that the Holy Spirit brings an electric atmosphere to make people tingle and go numb?

Hinn: Every time I welcome the Holy Spirit He opens the portals of heaven and ushers me into the presence of the Father (page 211).

Truth: According to the first quote, the Holy Spirit comes on demand to Benny. Then all he has to do is "welcome Him," and He ushers Benny Hinn into the presence of the Father. Not even the apostles Paul and John had continuous ushering into heaven, and they were personally selected by Jesus. How could anyone believe Mr. Hinn has more "ushering" favor with the Lord than the founding apostles (Ephesians 4:11-12)? Check online to see how often the word "portal" is used in occult teachings. Portal(s) access to heaven is not found in Scripture.

Hinn: The moment I touched this sorrowful woman, something remarkable took place. She broke into the most incredible laughter I'd ever seen, and she fell to the floor under God's power. Mr. Hinn also wrote that when her son tried to reach down and pull her up, "he fell to the floor laughing—just like his mother" (page 263).

Truth: Take plenty of time to read all of the Gospel healings where Jesus and His disciples ministered to people. There is not one instance recorded where they touched someone, and the person fell down with laughter because they were "under God's power." Throughout Scripture, God's power in healing or helping those afflicted in any way is to raise them up, not to knock them off their feet as they laugh their way to the floor. The circus entertainment of so-called "Holy laughter" while on the floor, seated, or standing is not found in any verse where the Holy Spirit ministers for the testimony of the real Jesus

Hinn: The Holy Spirit is a first-class Person who presents the Lord Jesus to the world with dignity, respect, and honor (page 264). God does not condone disorder (page 265).

Truth: The manifestations (dropping to the floor and shaking) Benny Hinn attributes to the Holy Spirit in his meetings cannot be found in any setting where Jesus or His disciples preached the true Word of God, and confirmed it with Holy Spirit power. When Jesus and His apostles healed, no Scripture teaches "people were slain in the spirit." Uncontrollable loss of physical stability to the point of hitting the floor is in direct opposition to what Paul wrote in 1 Corinthians 14:33—"For God is not the author of confusion." Uncontrollable laughs, drops, and shaking flops are confusing exhibitions which oppose the image of Christ, and are not attributed to any Holy Spirit gifts.

Benny Hinn: *Good Morning Holy Spirit*

I saw Jesus walk into my bedroom (page 20). You must understand that I did not know Jesus. I had not asked Christ to come into my heart. But the moment I saw Him, I recognized Him. I knew it was the Lord. When it happened, I was asleep, but suddenly my little body was caught up in an incredible sensation that can be only described as "electric." It felt as if someone had plugged me into a wired socket. There was a numbness that felt like needles—a million of them—rushing through my body.... The Lord didn't say anything to me. He just looked at me. And then He disappeared (page 21).

Truth: Would the real Jesus appear to someone who is not saved, say nothing about His Gospel of salvation, and just leave? This Jesus who brought "electric shock" and "needles" when he visited Benny sounds like "another Jesus," the type of counterfeit Jesus who is visiting for deception. There are no recorded New Covenant appearances of the Messiah where He simply appeared, looked at people, electrified them with numbness and needles, and left without saying a word.

Hinn: When I came out, she was thrown right back. Something had knocked her against the wall. I said, "What's wrong with you, Mama?" She answered, "I don't know." Well, the presence of the Lord almost knocked her down (page 40).

Truth: This presence of power that knocked his mother against the wall did not come from Jesus, the Prince of Peace (Isaiah 9:6). The Holy Spirit came to lead people to Jesus (John 15:26). He was not sent to beat up the Body of Christ. How can Benny Hinn entertain the thought that this presence which knocked his mother around was from the Lord? Does this seem like Holy Spirit power or "another spirit" power? People don't get physically abused in the loving presence of the Lamb of God.

Hinn: She called again, "Supper is ready." And as I was about to leave, I felt someone take my hand and say, "Five more minutes. Just five more minutes." The Holy Spirit longed for my fellowship (page 53).

Truth: This is a classic arrogant statement. Mr. Hinn portrays himself as a special man that the Holy Spirit *must* be around for fellowship. Since the Holy Spirit indwells all believers in Christ, He has plenty of time for fellowship with the millions who have Him within (Ephesians 1:13).

Hinn: Ministers on the platform and people in the audience felt the same thing—it was like a gust of wind that entered and swirled inside that place.... All over, people began to collapse and fall to the floor under the power of the Holy Ghost. They were "slain" in the Spirit (page 103).

Truth: When the Holy Spirit came at Pentecost while the disciples were praying, He did not "slay them in the spirit" with a gust of swirling wind. The Holy Spirit presence indicated they were filled with His Holiness, and standing upright they declared the testimony of Jesus (Acts 2:2-11, 38). Just the phrase "slain in the spirit" should alert our mind and heart that something is wrong with this belief. In Scripture, to slay means to kill! This bizarre behavior sounds more like a demonic encounter. The Holy Spirit does not spiritually electrify, knock unconscious for visual entertainment, make true believers shake uncontrollably, or pin people to the floor. He gives them life, a sound mind (2 Timothy 1:7), and keeps them spiritually upright. Being "slain in the Spirit" is *not* one of the "gifts of the Spirit" listed in 1 Corinthians 12:8-11, or any epistle!

E. W. Kenyon: *Jesus the Healer*

He is not talking about prayer. He is talking about casting out demons, about healing the sick, and miracles. Whatsoever ye shall demand in my name. That word "ask" means "demand" (page 21).

Truth: Mr. Kenyon is referring to John 14:13. He completely rejects the Greek word in the manuscript for "ask" (*aiteō*) in John 14:13, and replaces it with "demand" (*punthanomai*), a Greek word that is used in Matthew 2:4 and Acts 21:33. These two verses are examples of "demanding" information, not respectfully asking when addressing a person. Christians are never to demand anything from the LORD God! From the time the Holy Spirit came at Pentecost to Revelation 22:21, there is no record of Christians demanding of their Lord and Savior. Also, Mr. Kenyon puts words in the mouth of Jesus ("casting out demons, healing the sick, and miracles") that aren't found in John 14:13-14. This is sin (Proverbs 30:5-6), and Mr. Kenyon promoted "confession" and speaking "the Word of faith" (page 69).

Kenyon: All that foolish talk about Luke being Paul's physician is not true. Physicians were sorcerers. They belonged to the spiritualistic group (page 44).

Truth: In Colossians 4:14 Paul esteems Luke as "the beloved Physician," not the sorcerer. Mr. Kenyon chooses to reject clear Scripture which portrays Luke as God's beloved servant.

They Said it: Is it True?

Guillermo Maldonado: *Jesus Heals Your Sickness Today!*

From Genesis to Revelation, we read over and over again the confirmation of what has always been God's will: to heal His people (page 20).

Truth: Early in his book, Mr. Maldonado deceives the reader by saying it "has always been God's will to heal His people." God's people were not always healed according to Luke 4:27 where Jesus says there were "many lepers in Israel in the time of Elisha the prophet; and none of them was cleansed" except Namaan, the Syrian leper. John 5:2-9 records that many sought healing continually, but God only healed one person at specific times (verse 4). If it has always been God's will to heal his people, then Jesus should have healed all waiting at the pool. He didn't heal all because He only did His Father's will (John 4:34; 5:19-20; 6:38; 8:29). He also turned away multitudes who sought healing (Luke 5:15-16).

Guillermo Maldonado: *How to Walk in the Supernatural Power of God*

God started creating us in eternity and finished us before giving us the shape and form we have today. We arrived in the *now* via God's faith (page 108).

Truth: Genesis 2:7 teaches we were created from the dust of the ground on day six (Genesis 1:31), and God didn't use faith. Hasn't Mr. Maldonado read the first two chapters of the Bible?

Maldonado: Miracles should be everyday happenings, not isolated events (page 191). Miracles must be received and declared; otherwise, they will not stay (page 192).

Truth: The Lord Jesus did not teach that "miracles should be everyday happenings." Miracles occur according to God's will (1 Corinthians 12:10-11). Whenever Jesus or His disciples did a miracle, there was no declaration needed to keep the miracle. God's miracles last to verify He did it. If people lose a miracle, they never had it from God.

T. L. Osborn: *Healing The Sick*

A Moslem woman stood, listening to the message. Then, suddenly, she saw a great ball of light appear behind me on the podium. It burst, and then a huge open hand appeared behind me with blood dripping from it. She believed on the Lord Jesus Christ and was healed also. Another person saw a great light cover the field of people and a huge cross appeared. Then two pierced and bleeding hands appeared so large that they covered the entire audience. Blood sprayed from them over the people. Everyone who was engulfed in the flowing blood appeared to be immediately healed and made whole (pages 298-299). This vivid description is from a September, 1954, meeting held in Surabaja, Java, Indonesia.

Truth: A friend who came out of occult New Age teachings told me about the "ball of light" that appeared over his head while he was still in a New Age cult. No "great ball of light" ever appeared when Jesus or His apostles healed, and His blood did not drip out of the sky, spraying people to heal them. This supernatural event sounds more like an occult manifestation.

Osborn: Peter's wife was sick with a fever. And he [Jesus] stood over her and rebuked the fever; and it left her (Mark 1:30-31; Luke 4:39). You cannot rebuke something that cannot understand your words. You can rebuke only a personality (page 156).

Truth: Mr. Osborn is wrong for believing you can rebuke only a personality, because Jesus "rebuked the winds and the sea" in Matthew 8:26. There is no personality in wind or water. Mr. Osborn believes Peter's mother had a demon that caused her fever, yet Jesus did not rebuke the demon of fever. Whom will you believe, Lord Jesus or T. L. Osborn?

Dodie Osteen: *If My Heart Could Talk*

Mrs. Osteen teaches *It is God's will for you to be well* (page 127). However, her husband, John (1921-1999), "fought hypertension since he was in his forties," and had "emergency bypass surgery" in 1987 (page 196). Also, "his condition slowly worsened, his blood pressure remained elevated, and eventually his kidneys stopped functioning normally, so he began daily dialysis in 1998, three months before his death" (page 197). Though her husband suffered for years with different physical problems, she says this about Jesus; "He walked the shores of the Sea of Galilee and healed all who came to Him, and He still does it today" (pages 245-246).

Truth: If it is God's will for us to be well, why didn't the Lord Jesus heal her husband from his various ailments? The truth is found in Galatians 4:13, Philippians 2:25-29, 1 Timothy 5:23, and 2 Timothy 4:20. Jesus didn't heal all who came to Him (Luke 5:15-16), nor does He heal all the sick today.

Joel Osteen: *I Declare 31 Promises to Speak Over Your Life*

> **Truth:** The 31 days of "I Declare" listed in his book *declare* a major flaw in pastor Osteen's preaching. When studying the various verses modeled by Jesus and His disciples on prayer, asking, supplication, requests, and calling upon the LORD, there is no emphasis on a personal "I Declare" way of life. Why? Because this is declaring your future, which keeps Jesus out of first place in your life constantly. A careful check on how the word "declare" is used in the New Testament will show that the focus should not be on self-declarations of how I want my life to be. The focus should be on what Jesus declares for us.

Joel Osteen: *The Power of I AM*

> *Whatever follows the "I am" will eventually find you....* Get up in the morning and invite good things into your life (page 2). He then proceeds to instruct the reader on how to use "I am" seven times to "invite good things into your life."

> **Truth:** This is self-centered instruction that eliminates Jesus from first place (Colossians 1:18). When we arise, we should get up and praise God, give thanks, and pray for His guidance.

Osteen: You must prophesy health. Prophesy a long and productive life. Your words will become your reality (page 18). Talk about the way you want to be. You are prophesying your future (page 40).

Truth: Scripture does not instruct Christians to prophesy their future in any way. Mr. Osteen promotes too much focus on our words, rather than the LORD'S Word. Presumptuous prophecy is a great transgression (Psalm 19:13; James 4:13-15).

Osteen: If you struggle with your weight, declare, "I am in shape. I am healthy. I'm full of energy. I weigh what I should weigh." *It may not be true right now*, but you keep saying it and you're going to move toward it (page 42, emphasis mine).

Truth: This information reveals that Joel Osteen teaches his followers who have an obvious weight problem to live in denial of the truth. Denying the truth of physical evidence is a sin, and is a commonly found in false faith ministries.

Osteen: He is your Heavenly Father. You have His DNA. Imagine what you can do (page 77). I have the DNA of the Most High God (page 78). Now imagine that somehow we could do spiritual DNA testing.... You have His DNA. He created worlds. There's nothing too much for you. You can overcome that sickness.... It's no big deal for you to live healthy and whole.... It's in your spiritual DNA (page 79).

Truth: Pastor Osteen never cites a verse to verify that the LORD has spiritual DNA, because there is none. Within this false teaching about spiritual DNA, Joel Osteen uses the word "imagine" twice. Any imagination that exalts "itself against the knowledge of God" (2 Corinthians 10:5) is wrong! Pastor Osteen needs to forget about teaching people to "imagine" something about the LORD'S DNA and His children that is not Scriptural. Nowhere in any verse containing information on what happens when the Holy Spirit comes to indwell a person (Romans 8:9, 11) does it teach that we get God's Spiritual DNA *in* our DNA. A true understanding of the eternal God from Scripture reveals He never has, and never will co-mingle His nature with any created being! Our God does not convert us to spiritual hybrids at rebirth. He comes alongside within to give us eternal life and help renew us daily (Romans 12:2; 2 Corinthians 4:16). Teaching the unlearned and ignorant any false belief teaches them to bear false witness against the true God, and plants deception for failure in the future. This false teaching has the fragrance of "deep" New Age Mysticism.

Osteen: Every time you say, "I am anointed," chains are broken. Fear has to leave. Depression has to go. Healing comes. Strength comes. Faith comes (page 205).
Truth: No verse on "anointing" confirms any of these claims.

Joseph Prince: *Healing Promises*

To God, whether it's a new pimple on your face, a sore throat or an aching back, no matter how trivial or commonplace it sounds, if it troubles you, He wants to take care of it! (page 31).
Truth: Where is the Scripture to confirm God wants to take care of all trivial or commonplace things that bring discomfort? We are not guaranteed relief from *all* physical discomfort before we enter heaven. That comes later (Revelation 21:4-5). Look at Philippians 2:25-29, 1 Timothy 5:23, and 2 Timothy 4:20. These dedicated servants for Jesus were in much more pain and discomfort than what a pimple causes.

Jerry Savelle: *What I Learned from the men who imparted into me the most*

I once watched Brother Copeland minister to a man who had stomach cancer. Brother Copeland prayed until his faith reached its highest point, and then he laid hands on the man. Then Brother Copeland stood there for a while not saying a word. All of a sudden ... bam! He hit the man in the stomach, knocking him to the floor.... The man got up and declared he was healed, supposedly of stomach cancer. The next day he gave testimony that the proof of being healed was he could eat Mexican food again. (page 30).

Truth: If you read every Gospel setting where Jesus healed people, you will not find one account of Jesus slugging or striking anyone down to heal. His healing removed disease, and raised people "up" from their physical ailments.

Andrew Wommack: *God Wants You Well*

Paul was talking to his son in faith, Timothy, saying: *Drink no longer water, but use a little wine for thy stomach's sake and thine often infirmities (1 Timothy 5:23)*.... Apparently whatever sickness Timothy had was a stomach problem, and it was related to the water.... Paul was counseling Timothy to quit drinking the water because that's what was causing his stomach problems, and instead to drink a little wine. This isn't some endorsement for medicine.... No, it's very clear that this stomach problem was related to contaminated water (pages 69, 70, 71).

Truth: Mr. Wommack has a major problem with his teaching about 1 Timothy 5:23. The City of Ephesus, where Timothy was located, had a river flowing through it called the Cayster River, and it flowed into the Aegean Sea. There is no historical evidence stating this river had contaminated water flowing through it, making it undrinkable for all, when Timothy was at Ephesus. Paul doesn't say the water was contaminated, but Mr. Wommack's belief is contaminated with opposition to biblical truth. If the water was contaminated as Andrew Wommack teaches, why weren't other Christians and citizens having stomach problems? Paul does endorse "a little wine," not only for Timothy's stomach, but for Timothy's "often infirmities." Timothy had infirmities, as well as a stomach problem. So why didn't Andrew Wommack also explain Timothy's "often infirmities" in this verse? Ignoring an important part of this verse is not acceptable scholarship, and doesn't glorify Jesus.

Wommack: Laws are constant.... God doesn't violate natural laws. He doesn't violate spiritual laws either (page 131).

Truth: Every time Jesus did any miracle that changed or controlled the elements of His creation, He "violated" a natural law He created in the beginning of the world. The purpose of a statement like this is to get people to believe in spiritual laws of guarantee, such as health—"This truth directly applies to healing" (page 130). False teachers will tell listeners God has already provided for what they want. They just need to receive it "By faith." The LORD operates by His will, not spiritual laws. Jesus *never* taught spiritual laws for health or wealth.

Wommack: From an Andrew Wommack prayer: "*Father, we loose Your anointing to flow through their body to release them from pain and all these other symptoms*" (pages 169-170).

Truth: This prayer is a vivid picture of the authority some confused healers believe they possess. Nowhere in the Bible is it found that a Christian has authority to "loose" their heavenly Father's anointing to heal. It is God's anointing to loose.

False doctrines produce evidence that the teacher is not hearing from the LORD or discerning the Word of God properly (Romans 10:17). If a teaching goes against Scripture, it is *not* from the Holy Spirit of truth (John 14:17, 26). False teachings lead people to believe in "another Jesus" which produces an unacceptable gospel (2 Corinthians 11:3-4). False doctrine welcomes ongoing deception.

Endnotes:

1. Gloria Copeland, *God's Will is Prosperity* (Forth Worth, Texas: Kenneth Copeland Publications, 1978).
2. Kenneth Copeland, *The Laws of Prosperity* (Fort Worth, Texas: Kenneth Copeland Publications, 1974).
3. Creflo Dollar, *The Image of Righteousness You're More Than You Know* (Tulsa, OK: Harrison House Inc., 2002).

4. Jesse Duplantis, *Heaven—Close Encounters of the God Kind* (Tulsa, OK: Harrison House, 1996).

5. John Hagee, *The Power to Heal* (Dallas, Texas: Horticultural Printers, 1991).

6. John Hagee, *The Power of The Prophetic Blessing* (Brentwood, Tennessee: Worthy Publishing, 2012).

7. Kenneth Hagin, *How You Can Be Led By the Spirit of God, Legacy Edition* (Tulsa, Oklahoma: Kenneth Hagin Ministries, 2006).

8. Marilyn Hickey, *Your Pathway to Miracles* (New Kensington, PA: Whitaker House, 2011).

9. Benny Hinn, *Welcome, Holy Spirit* (Nashville, TN: Thomas Nelson, Inc., 1995).

10. Benny Hinn, *Good Morning Holy Spirit* (Nashville, TN: Thomas Nelson, Inc., 2004).

11. E. W. Kenyon, *Jesus the Healer* (Lynnwood, Washington: Kenyon's Gospel Publishing Society, 2010).

12. Guillermo Maldonado, *Jesus Heals Your Sickness Today!* (Miami, FL: ERJ Publicaciones, 2009).

13. Guillermo Maldonado, *How to Walk in the Supernatural Power of God* (New Kensington, PA: Whitaker House, 2011).

14. T. L. Osborn, *Healing The Sick* (Tulsa, Oklahoma: Harrison House, 1992).

15. Dodie Osteen, *If My Heart Could Talk* (New York, NY: FaithWords, 2016).

16. Joel Osteen, *I Declare 31 Promises to Speak Over Your Life* (New York, NY: FaithWords, 2012).

17. Joel Osteen, *The Power of I AM—Two Words That Will Change Your Life* (New York, NY: FaithWords, 2015).

18. Joseph Prince, *Healing Promises* (Lake Mary, Florida: Charisma House, 2012).

19. Jerry Savelle, *What I Learned from the men who imparted into me the most* (Crowley, Texas: Jerry Savelle Ministries International, 2014).

20. Andrew Wommack, *God Wants You Well* (Tulsa, Oklahoma: Harrison House Publishers, 2010).

Chapter 13

Did Jesus Die Twice?

More than fifty years ago, an unscriptural teaching about Christ's sacrificial death on the cross was planted on paper and in the ears of many. This false atonement doctrine has spread globally, and it *rejects* the shed blood of Jesus as being sufficient to forgive our sins. Those who believe Christ's physical death on the cross is *not* enough to forgive our sins say He must *also* die a spiritual death to complete His sacrifice. In order to establish what is called "the dual death" on the cross belief, E. W. Kenyon taught the following from Isaiah 53:9:

> The word "death," is plural in the Hebrew, indicating that Jesus died twice on the cross. He died spiritually the moment that God laid our Sin upon Him.[1]

We will look at the Hebrew word for "death" in Isaiah 53:9 which reads: "And He made His grave with the wicked, and with the rich in His death" to see if "death" is in the plural. If it is in the plural, does that mean Messiah Jesus died both physically and spiritually on the cross? Or does it have a specific Scriptural link to the horrible *physical* death Christ suffered?

From their *Isaiah Commentary*, scholars Keil and Delitzsch give us the needed understanding of the Hebrew word for "death."

> Thou shalt die the deaths of the uncircumcised by the hand of strangers: (Ezekiel 28:10). These scholars state that the plural form for "death" that is used in Isaiah 53:9 and Ezekiel 28:10 is a plur. Exaggerativus ... it is applied to a violent death, the very pain of which makes it like dying again and again.[2]

Nothing within the context of the Hebrew word for "death" in Isaiah 53:9 teaches the Messiah would die a spiritual *and* physical death on the cross. He bore our sin in His body (Hebrews 10:10), and He knew no sin spiritually (2 Corinthians 5:21; 1 Peter 2:22).

Isaiah used this Hebrew word for "death" in the plural form for a specific purpose; to inform us that the Messiah will suffer a violent and painful death, making it feel like He is dying repeatedly before finally dying. The One suffering would want to die because of the agony and pain, but could not die as quickly as desired. This is exactly what happened to Jesus while on the cross; "that He by the grace of God should taste death for every man" (Hebrews 2:9).

Plural nouns are common in Hebrew. They can be used to convey numerical plurality and/or "emphasize" a particular meaning of the word. Plural Hebrew nouns can also express intensity, amplification, magnitude, and multiplication of an idea.[3] For more understanding on the use of the Hebrew plural form, you can look at the work of E. Kautzsch and A. E. Cowley on pages 396-401 in their *Gesenius' Hebrew Grammar*.

If this "dual death" sacrifice by Jesus is true as some claim, why didn't even one New Testament author ever mention that Isaiah 53:9 foretold the "dual death" of the Messiah when writing about His sacrifice for our sins? Because the apostles knew the Hebrew language very well from their youngest days, they understood the proper teaching from Jesus concerning His sacrifice for the sins of the world (Luke 24:45-46). They knew there was no "dual death" occurrence at Calvary or in Hades. Will you accept this truth?

Did Jesus Suffer for Three Days in Hades?

There is no Scriptural evidence that Jesus suffered on the cross, and then needed to suffer for three additional days in Hades to complete the sacrifice for our sins. Yet, Word of Faith minsters have written and preached this for decades, as the following people teach:

Jesus bore sin into the pit of hell. He carried it into the region of the damned to do away with sin![4] (Capps).

Because He tasted Spiritual death for every man, His spirit, His inner man, went to hell in our place[5] (Hagin).

He was made sin, was under condemnation and for three days and nights he was in Hell, locked up in the Prison House of Death[6] (Kenyon).

He is to put Sin away.... He could not do that in His physical life[7] (Kenyon).

When Jesus died, His spirit was taken by the Adversary, and carried to the place where the sinner's spirit goes when he dies[8] (Kenyon).

Colossians 2:15 gives a description of a battle that took place in Hades before Jesus arose from the dead[9] (Kenyon).

Satan had conquered Jesus on the Cross ... All the sufferings and torments that Hell could produce were heaped upon Jesus. When He had suffered Hell's agonies for three days and nights, the Supreme Court of the Universe cried, "Enough"[10] (Kenyon).

He was in the grave three days. During that time, He entered hell and defeated Satan.... He committed His Spirit to the Father and died. So they put Him, His body, in a grave, and His Spirit went to hell because that is where we deserved to go[11] (Meyer).

No verses accompany any of these quotes proclaiming that Jesus must suffer in Hades, because there aren't any. These quotes confirm that Charles Capps, Kenneth E. Hagin, E. W. Kenyon, Joyce Meyer, and many Word-Faith followers have a completely unscriptural view of Christ's death on the cross, and what transpired during the three days His body was in the tomb. Haven't they read the Gospel accounts where details are given concerning the crucifixion death of the Lord Jesus? In John 19:30, before Jesus dies, He says "It is finished." Jesus said His death finished His Father's requirement for the forgiveness of our sins! There was no need to go to Hades and be tortured by Satan for three more days to finalize the sacrifice of forgiveness.

Furthermore, the veil in the temple was rent/split from the top to the bottom *when* the Messiah died (Matthew 27:51; Mark 15:38), indicating the sacrifice was finished. No Scripture teaches that the Messiah must be crucified (suffer) on the cross, and then He must suffer three additional days of punishment from Satan in Hades so our sins can be forgiven. The blood Christ shed on the cross provides our forgiveness/sanctification (Matthew 26:28; Romans 3:24-25; 5:9; Ephesians 1:7; Colossians 1:14, 20; Hebrews 13:12; 1 Peter 1:18-19).

Though immeasurable pain, agony, and suffering were constant on the cross, it is the blood of Jesus that cleanses us from all sin (1 John 1:7). Christ's body alone (Hebrews 10:5, 10), not His spirit also (there is no blood in His spirit), was the offering His Father desired for our sanctification. His body "bare our sins" (1 Peter 2:24).

Isaiah 53:4 declares that the Messiah would be "smitten of God," not by Satan and his demons. Nothing in Isaiah 53 or any Gospel crucifixion account reveals that Satan took Christ's spirit to Hades for three days of ongoing suffering before our sins could be forgiven. Also, Paul writes in 1 Corinthians 15:3 that Christ died for our sins according to the Scriptures. Paul does not write that Christ died *twice* for our sins, and Paul got the Gospel directly from Jesus (Galatians 1:11-12).

Those who believe Jesus battled Satan and his demons in Hades to finalize our forgiveness are 100% wrong. He made an open and public triumph with His victory over sin and Satan on the cross (Colossians 2:14-15). Before leaving this section, clarification is needed for unraveling three verses used to teach people that Jesus spent three days in Hades being tortured by demons.

In Matthew 12:40, Jesus talks about the Son of Man spending three days and nights in the heart of the earth. Jesus is foretelling His death and physical resurrection. He does not say one word about suffering for the sins of the world in Hades during these three days.

John 20:17 reveals that He had not ascended to His Father in His new, glorified body. Again, not one word of undergoing three days of satanic beatings in Hades.

When Peter preaches at Pentecost, he says Jesus of Nazareth was not abandoned in hell (Hades), and His body would not see corruption (Acts 2:27). Since we know His body was in the tomb for three days, where was Christ's spirit during this time?

W. E. Vine's *Expository Dictionary of New Testament Words* provides vital insight for understanding Hades, which will clarify the location of Jesus' spirit while His body awaited the resurrection:

> the region of departed spirits of the lost (but including the blessed dead in periods preceding the Ascension of Christ).[12]

In Luke 16:19-31, Jesus presents explicit information from a parable called "The rich man and Lazarus." He describes Hades in verses 23-24 as a place of "torments" and "flame" for the selfish rich man, and a place of comfort for Lazarus in Abraham's bosom. Apparently Jewish thought at this time viewed Hades as a divided place, a place of spiritual torment for the evil people awaiting God's judgment, and a place of spiritual comfort (Paradise) for those with whom God was pleased.

When Jesus was crucified, He told one of the criminals on the cross that they would be together "in Paradise" *on the day* when both were crucified (Luke 23:42-43). To fulfill His word to the criminal, Jesus must go to the Paradise section of Hades, not the section of torment for more suffering! This teaches that *after* Jesus committed His spirit to His Father (Luke 23:46), He was sent by His Father to Paradise, not to Satan's presence to finalize the blood atonement.

Years pass after Pentecost and Peter writes in his epistle that Jesus was "put to death in the flesh, but quickened by the Spirit" (1 Peter 3:18). Peter does not say the Holy Spirit quickened Christ's dead, sin-filled spirit that was tormented in Hades. This statement refers to His body (flesh) being quickened to be resurrected. Long after Peter's first message recorded in Acts 2, he still preaches and writes about the physical death of Jesus. Peter does not record anything about Christ dying *spiritually* on the cross or being *tormented* in Hades.

The apostles understood the Hebrew language very well, and they knew the proper teaching from Jesus concerning His sacrifice for the sins of the world (Luke 24:45-46). They knew there was no "dual death" occurrence at Calvary or in Hades. The "dual death atonement" belief tells Jesus His shed blood is not sufficient to forgive our sins. Would you tell Jesus His blood is *not sufficient* to forgive your sins?

Was Jesus Born-Again in Hades?

Worldwide faith literature teaches that Jesus needed to be born-again in hell before He was resurrected. Here is their unsound doctrinal belief:

> But Jesus, the Son of God, arose—born again of the Spirit of God[13] (Capps).

> It was the third day down in the Prison House of Death that He was Born Again of the Spirit. That was His New Birth[14] (Kenyon).

He was the first born out of spiritual death, the first person who was ever born again[15] (Kenyon).

This is a remarkable fact, that Jesus was born again before He was raised from the dead[16] (Kenyon).

In other words Paul saw Him Born Again in the dark regions where He had been suffering the torments of the damned for man[17] (Kenyon). Paul *never* wrote anything like this!

Holding true to heretical form, these two men don't back any of their doctrine with Scripture. To test the accuracy of the teaching that Jesus was born-again in Hades, let's read the Scriptural teaching on being born-again. In John 3:3, Jesus begins explaining the words "born-again" (spiritual rebirth) when talking to a Pharisee named Nicodemus. Jesus is referring to seeing the kingdom of God (verse 3), and entering the kingdom of God (verse 5) when born-again (verse 7).

For spiritual rebirth to occur, you must admit (confess) you have sinned (Romans 3:23), believe Jesus is God's only Savior for all humanity (Acts 4:10-12), and believe His shed blood on the cross cleanses you from all your sins (Matthew 26:27-28). In receiving forgiveness from Jesus, you must also believe God raised Him from the dead and confess Him as Lord (Romans 10:9-10). This example of becoming born-again was meant to show whether Jesus qualifies as a sinner who needs to be born-again.

Did Jesus ever sin? The apostle Peter knew Him well and says "No" in 1 Peter 2:22, and Paul says that though He was made sin (in His body) for us, *He knew no sin* (2 Corinthians 5:21). To *know* sin, a person would have to engage in sin, thereby willfully sinning against God and fulfilling Romans 3:23. Jesus never sinned against His Father or anyone. Did Jesus ever ask His Father to forgive His sins so He could be born-again? Do you see how unbiblical this "Jesus was born-again in hell" teaching is?

Scripture is clear that Jesus was not and did not need to be born-again in Hades. Satan must be delighted to hear people give him credit for doing things to Jesus which he did not do, or is *not* capable of doing. No verse says Christ's heavenly Father gave Satan authority *over* Jesus to drag His spirit into Hades and punish Him for three days. Nor does any verse teach Jesus had to be born-again before He could be resurrected. And Jesus never told His disciples He was born-again in Hades. People who teach this false doctrine need to examine themselves to see if *the real* Jesus dwells in them (2 Corinthians 13:5).

Are Christians Incarnations of God Like Jesus?

For some false faith ministers, it is not good enough for them to claim they are gods, which they aren't. They teach the following as truth:

> Every man who has been born-again is an Incarnation. The believer is as much an Incarnation as was Jesus of Nazareth.[18]

To say Christians are incarnations of Jesus is ridiculous, because no Scripture supports this teaching. In John 3:3-7, Jesus explains to Nicodemus what it means to be born-again. He does not teach Nicodemus that when he becomes born-again, he would be an incarnation of Messiah. Also, in all *The Book of Acts* messages, the apostles *never* taught new believers they were incarnations of Jesus.

Let's look at some of Christ's qualities and historical events that took place in His life and eternal existence. Then we can see if any Christian qualifies as an incarnation of Jesus. The word "incarnation" means "in the flesh" or "embodied in flesh," and in this case it means Jesus pre-existed and came from heaven to dwell upon the earth:

1. Jesus existed with His Father in the beginning of creation (John 1:1-3), and His days are from everlasting (Micah 5:2).

Can any Word of Faith believer prove living in heaven before living on the earth?

2. John 1:14 says the Word, Jesus, became flesh and dwelt among us. This indicates he had another nature prior to becoming flesh and living among us. That "another" nature was, is, and will always be the same eternal spiritual (essence) nature like His eternal Father. Can any faith teacher prove he or she had an eternal nature prior to being born in the flesh?

3. Since the main purpose of Christ incarnating was to save people from their sins so they could be in heaven with Him, the teaching stating "All Christians are incarnations of Jesus" *trivializes* the work and Person of our Savior. This definition reduces the humbling impact of God becoming a man (John 1:1-14), coming to earth to die for our sins, and be resurrected.

Scripture in this chapter verifies: 1) Jesus did not die spiritual *and* physical deaths on the cross for our sins, *and* did not take our sins to Hades in His spirit to complete the atonement. Messiah's body was sufficient to bear our sins. 2) Jesus' spirit was *not* tormented in Hades for three days by demons to complete the sacrifice for our sins. His blood sacrifice for our sins was completed on the cross. 3) Jesus was *not* born-again in the torments section of Hades, because the torments section (Luke 16:20-31) is for non-repentant sinners. They don't get out and ascend to heaven. 4) Christians are *not* incarnations of God like Jesus.

Endnotes:
1. E. W. Kenyon, *What Happened from the Cross to the Throne* (Lynnwood, Washington: Kenyon's Gospel Publishing Society, 2010), p. 43.

2. C. F. Keil and Franz Delitzsch, *Commentary on the Old Testament*, Volume 7, *Isaiah* (Grand Rapids, Michigan: William B. Eerdmans Publishing Company, 1978), Part II, p. 329.

3. E. Kautzsch, edited and enlarged. Translated by A. E. Cowley, *Gesenius' Hebrew Grammer* (Mineola, New York: Dover Publications, Inc., 2006), pp. 396-401.

4. Charles Capps, *Authority in Three Worlds* (Tulsa, Oklahoma: Harrison House, 1982), p. 155.

5. Kenneth Hagin, *The Name of Jesus* (Tulsa, Oklahoma: Kenneth Hagin Ministries, 1979), p, 29.

6. E. W. Kenyon, *Jesus the Healer* (Lynnwood, Washington: Kenyon's Gospel Publishing Society, 2010), p. 82.

7. E. W. Kenyon, *What Happened from the Cross to the Throne* (Lynnwood, Washington: Kenyon's Gospel Publishing Society, 2010), p. 47.

8. Ibid., p. 47.

9. Ibid., p. 65.

10. Ibid., p. 89.

11. Joyce Meyer, *The Most Important Decision You Will Ever Make* (New York, NY: Warner Faith, 2003), pp. 31, 32.

12. W. E. Vine, *An Expository Dictionary of New Testament Words* (Old Tappan, New Jersey: Fleming H. Revell Company, 1966), Vol. II, E-Li, p. 187.

13. Capps, *Authority in Three Worlds,* p. 144.

14. Kenyon, *Jesus the Healer,* p. 82.

15. Kenyon, *What Happened from the Cross to the Throne,* p. 62.

16. Ibid., p. 64.

17. Ibid., p.116.

18. E. W. Kenyon, *The Bible in the Light of our Redemption* (Lynnwood, Washington: Kenyon's Gospel Publishing Society, 1995), p. 151.

Chapter 14

Misrepresenting the Blood of Christ

The distortion of what Christ's blood truly represents has expanded to various ministries globally. New interpretations about what the blood of Christ represents have surfaced. People are partaking of The Lord's Table (Communion) with the belief that Jesus taught "doing this in remembrance of Me" provides physical healing. Also, there is a popular power and authority belief known as "Dominionism" or "Dominion Theology." The biblically ignorant find this doctrine appealing, because they are told the blood of Jesus gives them complete healing, prosperity, and authority/dominion on every place their foot treads.

We will look at "Dominion Theology" first to see if it was taught in the New Covenant. Then we will move on to establishing the true meaning of The Lord's Supper.

Was Christ's Blood Shed for Christian Dominion?

There are those who teach that when Jesus shed His blood from seven specific areas on His body, His blood gave "dominion" (control) over to 7 specific areas in the believer's life. Some refer to this doctrine as "Dominion Theology." It has become widespread among Word-Faith participants. We will investigate their belief and compare these 7 areas to what the Lord taught on His blood. I will be citing information from pastor Larry Huch's book, *The 7 Places Jesus Shed His Blood* (2004 edition).[1]

1. The first place Jesus shed His blood was in the Garden of Gethsemane on the night of the Last Supper with His disciples. It's not a coincidence that the first place Jesus ransomed us or shed His redemptive blood was in a garden, because the first

place we lost the power of God's blessing was in another garden, the Garden of Eden (page 23).

Immediately, it's quite obvious that pastor Huch doesn't honor Scripture as it was recorded. His teaching that Jesus "shed" His blood in the Garden of Gethsemane is refuted by Luke 22:44 which reads, "And being in an agony He prayed more earnestly; and His *sweat* was as it were great drops of blood falling down to the ground" (emphasis mine). Luke doesn't write that Jesus *shed* His redemptive blood and ransomed us in the Garden of Gethsemane. Luke writes that Jesus *sweat* drops of blood. Pastor Huch's entire doctrine of *his* "7 fold shed blood dominion blessing" falls apart instantly. But he doesn't seem to care about the truth of Luke 22:44. As you'll see, he continues in teachings 2-7 to ignore and misrepresent God's Holy Scripture, thus not honoring Christ's blood properly.

2. The second place Jesus shed His blood was at the whipping post (page 37). On page 38 he says, "If Jesus suffered the whip for our healing, of course it is His will we be healed."

He quotes Isaiah 53:5 (page 37) to establish his doctrinal position that the 39 stripes Jesus took on His back were for our physical healing. Isaiah 53:5 clearly mentions "transgressions, iniquities, and chastisement for our peace." These words signify spiritual healing needs, not physical healing. Nothing is said about physical healing of disease or sickness in Isaiah 53:5. The only place Isaiah 53:5 is mentioned in the New Testament is 1 Peter 2:24, and Peter records it to teach *spiritual* healing, *not* physical healing, for those who had strayed from and returned to the Shepherd of their souls (verse 25).

3. We are redeemed by the precious blood of Jesus. Through His blood, we have been brought back to the state Adam and Eve enjoyed in the Garden of Eden (page 50). On page 51, pastor

Huch says "The symbol of poverty was placed on the brow of Jesus, the second Adam. When those thorns pierced His brow, He shed His blood for our redemption from poverty. We were cursed with poverty by the sweat of Adam's brow, but we were redeemed from the curse of poverty by the blood on Jesus' brow."

Jesus didn't teach "brow poverty redemption," nor did His apostles. The first century Christians never were "brought back to the state Adam and Eve enjoyed in the Garden of Eden." This doctrine is fabricated, an invention from someone who is not connected with the proper context of God's Scripture. When talking about the blood of Jesus, what verse teaches that the crown of thorns placed on His forehead would redeem us from poverty? Does Jesus remind the church in Revelation 2:9 that His bloody crown of thorns redeemed them from the curse of poverty? Furthermore, when Adam was driven out of the Garden, he was not in a state of material poverty. He had the entire earth to meet his needs, and it met the needs of the many who increased the earth's population.

4. The fourth place Jesus' blood was shed was from His hands, where the soldiers pounded spikes to nail Him to the cross. I believe that through the blood shed from His nail-pierced hands, God says everything we put our hands to He will cause to prosper. (See Genesis 39:3).

This doctrine found on page 72 is absurd, truly illogical when one looks at Genesis 39:2-3. These verses reveal the LORD was with Joseph and made all that he did "to prosper in his hand." There is *nothing* in the context of Genesis 39:3 to connect it with the blood that will come out of the Lord's nail-pierced hands, which would cause Christians to prosper. Are you seeing how unbiblical "Dominion Theology" is in an effort to claim money through the blood of Jesus?

Those who use the sin-forgiving blood of Jesus for monetary gain are redefining and presenting His blood in a way His apostles never did!

5. The fifth place where Jesus shed His blood was where they drove the spikes through His feet, nailing Him to the cross. The blood shed from His feet also redeemed us from our loss of dominion and authority.... Every place on which the sole of your foot treads shall be yours. (Deuteronomy 11:24).

On page 78, Larry Huch chose to not quote the entire verse, and when the rest of the verse is presented you will know why. This word from the LORD (verse 24) was spoken to Moses, and includes the area "from the wilderness and Lebanon, from the river, the river Euphrates, even unto the uttermost sea shall your coast be." This information from God is *not* for New Covenant believers giving them the right to claim dominion and authority wherever the sole of their foot treads. It is foretelling specifically what land God will give to the Israelites as they obey Him, and no man will be able to stand before them, because God will drive out the nations (verse 23). The unstable and untaught (2 Peter 3:16) will go to unbiblical extremes to find a verse for prosperity or personal authority that fits their "Dominion Theology."

6. The sixth place Jesus shed His blood was where a soldier shoved a spear into His side and blood and water poured out. Jesus died so that we could be forgiven (page 87). Next, he quotes Luke 4:18 (page 88) which describes the Messiah's ministry. Then he cites Nehemiah 8:10 (page 89) which says, "The joy of the LORD is your strength." From these two verses, he moves on to Proverbs 6:30-31 where it talks about a thief who steals because he is starving, and says the thief is the devil, which is not true. In this verse, the thief is a person (page 89). Finalizing his multiple mistakes, pastor Huch says according to Proverbs 6:30-31 the devil "has to pay you back sevenfold."

(page 89). The joy the enemy has stolen from you must be returned to you sevenfold (page 90).

An unbeliever without the indwelling Holy Spirit could see the fallacy in his pogo stick Scripture use. Why are so many, who claim to be born-again and Spirit-filled, accepting this doctrine as from the LORD? The apostles never taught the reason Jesus was speared in His side was to return sevenfold joy to all who believed in Him.

7. The seventh place Jesus shed His blood was in His bruises (page 103).

Pastor Larry Huch says since Isaiah 53:5 teaches Jesus "was bruised for our iniquities" it refers to some of our bruises that go deep, and God will forgive what we have done, heal our spiritually bruised areas, and give us the power on the inside to walk in total victory (pages 103, 104). Yes, our God does provide and offer forgiveness (spiritual healing) to any who repent and seek the LORD with a pure heart.

Though a little truth was found in these seven areas, the *large amount* of error (false doctrine, 1 John 2:21) convicts "Dominion Theology" of sinning against the blood of Jesus by adding to the meaning of His blood (Proverbs 30:5-6). In the New Covenant, the real Jesus didn't teach His blood was to be used for "dominion domination" in 7 different areas of our Christian life. At the cross, His eternal blood dominion (salvation) over the consequences of sin was shown to the world. Do you need to repent concerning your belief about the precious blood of Jesus?

Does Communion Guarantee Physical Healing?

Joseph Prince wrote a book titled *Health And Wholeness Through The Holy Communion.*[2] We will look at several quotes from his 2015 edition to biblically test his Communion teachings with what Jesus and Paul taught. The following quotes will verify pastor Prince's teaching position on health and healing for all in The Lord's Supper (Holy Communion):

1. The Holy Communion—God's Channel Of Divine Health (page 7).

2. God has since shown me that the body and blood should not be treated as one.... The wine, which is His blood, is for our forgiveness. And the bread, which is His body, is for our healing (page 24).

3. Because of what He did at the cross, we do not have just forgiveness, we also have healing. Forgiveness and healing go hand in hand (page 36).

4. Paul said, "*For as often as you eat this bread and drink this cup, you proclaim the Lord's death till He comes.*" (1 Corinthians 11:26, page 42).

5. But if you are sick, I would recommend that you have Communion daily (page 45).

6. In this case, "unworthily" describes the action of eating and drinking. It is not describing the person who is drinking or eating (page 52).

7. The Corinthians partook unworthily because they did not recognize that the broken body of the Lord was meant to bring them health and wholeness (page 53).

8. So Paul was not saying that if you have sin in your life, you cannot partake. He was telling them to partake in the correct manner, which is to recognize that the Lord's body was broken so that ours can be made whole (pages 54-55).

9. So as you partake, release your faith in the bread and the wine. Hold the bread in your hand and say this: "Thank you Jesus for Your broken body. It is for my healing, my spouse's healing and my children's healing. Thank You that by Your stripes, by the beatings You bore, by the lashes that fell on Your back, we are completely healed. I believe and I receive" (page 64).

Reread these nine excerpts carefully. Joseph Prince has rejected what Jesus and Paul taught about The Lord's Table. He believes Holy Communion is "God's Channel of Divine Health." This is not true, because we have gifts of healings (1 Corinthians 12:9) to represent God's will in healing, as well as the elder's prayers of faith (James 5:14-16). Jesus never taught His Table was "God's Channel of Divine Health" as confirmed by Matthew 26:26-28, Mark 14:22-24, and Luke 22:19-20. And Jesus never taught His sacrifice and shed blood guaranteed healing for all in this life. When done in remembrance of the Lord, it is to *proclaim* His death (1 Corinthians 11:26) which cleanses us from all the consequences of sin. Paul does not record that Communion is to proclaim physical healing for all, and Paul didn't recommend that the sick take Communion daily to get healed.

In number 6, pastor Prince shows his lack of understanding common English action with adverbs. You can't separate the verbal action of the words from the mouth of the person who said them. We are responsible for every word that comes out of our mouth (Matthew 12:36). If you are in sin, you are unworthy to partake of The Lord's Table until you repent. His rejection of the extreme importance of a clean/repentant heart *before* partaking of Communion reveals that he believes it doesn't matter if you have sin in your life. Such a position teaches his followers to disregard the proper purpose of Holy Communion. It's called *Holy* because we are to honor the Holy One of Israel, the Messiah, with repentant hearts when partaking.

Verses 28-30 show the importance of *examining* ourselves to confess any sin in our lives. Those who partake in Communion with active or unconfessed sin reject the cleansing power of Christ's blood (1 John 1:9), and turn it into *unholy Communion* with preordained consequences (verse 30).

Pastor Cho and The Fourth Dimension

In the late 70s, a Korean pastor named David Yonggi Cho wrote a book titled *The Fourth Dimension*[3] which caused great concern among many in Christ worldwide. When pastor Cho wrote his book, he had congregation members of over 730,000 in more than 25,000 home cell groups (back cover). As you read the forthcoming information on The Fourth Dimension, you will know why there should always be a great concern over this book, and his Volume Two.

On pages 25-28, he mentions people in Korea such as Buddhist monks, Japanese Sokagakkai, and those in Yoga meditation are being healed of stomach ulcers, the deaf and dumb are hearing and speaking, and the blind are seeing. He says their healings come from their faith as it incubates in "the fourth dimension."

Pastor Cho also teaches that the Holy Spirit "belongs to the fourth dimension. So the spiritual kingdom of faith belongs to the fourth dimension" (page 27). This is a ridiculous statement, an insult to the Holy Spirit. He goes on to say that "we can link our spirit's fourth dimension to the fourth dimension of the Holy Father," and "we can have all the more dominion over circumstances" (page 29). No verse says the Holy Spirit shares a spiritual realm with demonic healing powers, or that our human spirit is linked to the spiritual Fourth Dimension.

He believes "Visions and dreams are the language of the fourth dimension" (page 31). Also, he encourages an occult belief by suggesting creative visualization: "Through visualizing and dreaming you can incubate your future and hatch the results" (page 32). He adds to the Genesis 2:7 account of God creating man by stating that "When God created us, He created in us the fourth dimension, the spiritual world" (page 35). There is no verse in the creation account saying God "created *in* us the fourth dimension."

Without ever citing a biblical reference, he continues to say "I can go into the fourth dimension of the Holy Spirit, and I tell Him what is needed in my church in Korea, and He carries out the work" (page 36). Pastor Cho continues to make up things about the Almighty God that are not found in the Bible by stating, "Throughout Scripture God always made use of this law of the fourth dimension" (page 47). The phrase, "law of the fourth dimension" is never found in Scripture!

Since the Bible doesn't confirm any of Mr. Cho's "fourth dimension" teachings, let's learn how the occult describes The Fourth Dimension.

The Occult Fourth Dimension

The following resources will show clearly what constitutes The Fourth Dimension, and what transpires in this spiritual realm. This should convince *all* people to stay out of it.

THE FOURTH DIMENSION
The Truth ... The Astral Plane

The Fourth Dimension is a gray, polarized plane, housing the forces of Light and Darkness. The battle between good and evil starts here. Forms naturally morph on the Astral Plane ... Shamans are adept in this arena ... Magic, time travel, karma, reincarnation, luck, psychic surgery, flying, mind reading, disembodied spirits, enchantment, and of course, astral travel, all source from this plane.... The Demi-God/desses of many religions live here. Hell and purgatory are fourth dimensional locales as well.[4] (This is a demonic realm, filled with evil!). **Insight:** We are told to abstain from all evil (Romans 13:12; 1 Thessalonians 5:22). This clear information on The Fourth Dimension portrays it as an extremely wicked demonic realm.

The fourth dimension is the lowest level of the Spirit World and it is divided into the Astral Realm and the Realm of Hell.[5]
Insight: True Christians spend time in prayer that is directed to the LORD in heaven. Why would Christians have any "creative visualization" contact with The Fourth Dimension realm, talk to the spirit world, or the Realm of Hell *if* they are born-again?

In this chapter, we learned that many who claim to be Christians are not honoring the precious blood of Jesus according to Scripture (false Dominion Theology and a wrong Communion belief). This is a serious sin. Repent quickly. And if needed, renounce all involvement with The Fourth Dimension. Always keep a clean heart before Jesus.

Endnotes:

1. Larry Huch, *The 7 Places Jesus Shed His Blood* (New Kensington, PA: Whitaker House, 2004).
2. Joseph Prince, *Health And Wholeness Through The Holy Communion* (Printed in the United States of America, 2015).
3. Dr. David Yonggi Cho, *The Fourth Dimension Volume One* (Alachua, Florida: Bridge-Logos, 1979).
4. This website information can be found by typing in the heading of the article or typing; Description Of The Third, Fourth And Fifth Dimensions.
5. http://www.happy-science.org/the-truth-of-the-spirit-world

In *Jesus Heals Your Sickness Today*, Guillermo Maldonado also confirms his belief in The Fourth Dimension as of the LORD. He calls it "the dimension of eternity or glory" (page 159). Evil spirits are in The Fourth Dimension, and no Scripture defines The Fourth Dimension as "the LORD' S dimension of eternity or glory." The true God (John 17:3) doesn't *share* the same spiritual realm with demons.

Chapter 15

Matthew 8:17 Explains Isaiah 53:4

For over fifty years, multitudes have been taught that Isaiah 53:4 verifies Jesus died to redeem us from all sickness, griefs and sorrows, just as He died to redeem us from all our sins. Benny Hinn is one of many worldwide faith healers who teaches Isaiah 53:4 guarantees healing, and he connects it to Matthew 8:16-17 for proof.[1] Isaiah 53:4 will be listed first, then Matthew 8:17:

> Surely He hath borne our griefs, and carried our sorrows: yet we did esteem Him stricken, smitten of God, and afflicted.

> That it might be fulfilled which was spoken by Isaiah the prophet, saying, Himself took our infirmities, and bare our sicknesses.

Isaiah 53:4 refers to Christ's time on the cross, whereas Matthew 8:17 refers to a specific time in Christ's healing ministry *before* the cross. To properly understand the difference between these verses is essential for discerning the work of Jesus on the cross, and His work in His earthly healing ministry. Since many are taught that the blood of animals was used in the Old Covenant for physical healing, we will check that belief first to see if it is true.

Old Covenant Insight on Atonement Healing

F. F. Bosworth (1877-1958) taught: "As in Leviticus the types show that healing was invariably through atonement, so Matthew 8:16-17 definitely states that Christ healed all diseases on the ground of the atonement."[2] This quote teaches physical healing was provided for the Old Covenant people in Leviticus. Therefore, we can expect to be healed by Jesus "on the ground of His atonement." But did Mr. Bosworth teach the truth about the animal blood in Leviticus, or did he teach and author false doctrine on both covenant atonements?

Leviticus 14:18-19 teaches us about making atonement for cleansing, but it is important to understand what the atonement represents. Throughout Leviticus 13 leprosy is discussed. The priest *continues* to check the leper and his garments to see *if* the disease has been healed. When the leper is brought before the priest (Leviticus 14:2), "if the plague of leprosy be healed in the leper" (verse 3), then the priest shall give orders to prepare the cleansing sacrifices and atonement (verses 4-19). Notice the word "if" in verse 3. If the leper is healed, it is time to prepare the sin offering (verse 13).

Verse 3 gives us the key to refuting "the atonement provides healing teaching." The priest cannot command the wave offering and sacrifice to be given *until* the leper is healed. The atonement offering comes *after* the leper has been healed, and does not *cause* the leprosy to be cured. The "if" in verse 3 lets the priest know whether he should command preparation for the wave, sin, and guilt offerings (verses 12-14). Verse 19 verifies that the atonement is to cleanse the person's sin.

If atonement in the Old Covenant is the means of physical healing as some faith healers teach, then why does the priest have to repeatedly check the leper as recorded in Leviticus 13? He should just make the blood atonement for sin, and then healing will occur. However, the priest knew Mosaic Law did *not* teach that the blood of animals guaranteed physical healing for the sick and diseased. In obedience to the LORD, the priest honored the meaning of the blood and did not "add" anything to what the LORD said it represented for the people.

What Did Jesus Teach about Old Covenant Healing?

In Luke 4:27, Jesus teaches that there were many lepers in Israel in the time of Elisha the prophet and none of them was cleansed, but only

Naaman the Syrian. This statement from Jesus presents a big problem for those who believe healing came through atonement in the Old Covenant, because all lepers in Israel were not being healed or cleansed during the time of Elisha, yet atonement was made annually.

This indicates that atonement was made for the sins, iniquities, and transgressions of the people, *not* for healing the diseases of the people as recorded in Leviticus 16:3, 5, 6, 9, 11, 15, 16, 21, 22, 27, 30, and 34. Never is it cited in Leviticus 16 that the annual sacrifice was for healing *all* physical sickness and disease.

Matthew 8:1-3 records Jesus healing a leper. In verse 4, Jesus tells the cleansed man to go show himself to the priest and make the offering Moses taught. Leviticus 13-14:2 gives proof that leprosy was cleansed without atonement. By healing this leper, Jesus showed it was not by Old Covenant atonement that one received physical healing, but by the grace of God.

There were many sick and diseased Jews during Christ's ministry. What kept them from being healed if all they had to do was rely on the Old Covenant atonement for healing? If atonement healing was guaranteed, Jesus, Who knew the Law well, could have reminded the priests to tell the sick that the atonement would heal all their sickness. Constant or annual miraculous healings could have made an impression unto salvation among some of the heathens.

Also, Jesus healed only one man at the pool of Bethesda (John 5:2-9), a man with an infirmity for 38 years. If atonement healing was guaranteed, why hadn't this man found out for 38 years? Certainly there were some Pharisees and a high priest who knew what the annual atonement for sins meant, and if it guaranteed healing. If healing was for all in the Old Covenant, why didn't Jesus tell those in need of healing to remind the priest they wanted to be healed through the atonement? The answer is obvious; Jesus knew physical healing *was not* guaranteed through the Old Covenant atonement. Christians should think and talk like Jesus.

We should accept that Jesus *selected* only one person among the multitude who sought healing in this setting. The others displayed public faith to receive, saw a miracle, but did not receive one. Keep this in mind to have the true Holy Spirit understanding about the healing ministry of Jesus.

John the Baptist was a great prophet (Luke 7:28) and knew what the Old Covenant atonement represented. When the Word of God came to John the Baptist, he preached "the baptism of repentance for the remission of sins" (Luke 3:2-3). John did not teach the baptism of repentance, healing, and money for all through the Messiah's coming atonement.

A popular Old Testament Scripture used to promote faith healing is Psalm 103:3. The psalmist records that the LORD is the One Who forgives and pardons all of our iniquities and heals all of our diseases. Some people say this verse is proof God will heal all our diseases and every sickness if we ask Him with faith from our heart. However, we just learned from Jesus that God didn't always cleanse or heal in the Old Covenant (Luke 4:27). Specifically, what is the Holy Spirit saying to us in Psalm 103:3?

From their *Psalms Commentary*, Keil and Delitzsch give the answer. Above verse 1 in The *Fourth Book Of The Psalter* it reads:

Hymn In Honour Of God The All-Compassionate One.[3]

This Psalm is a Hymn people sing to glorify, honor, and praise God as recorded in verse 1. It does not establish a doctrinal guarantee that God will heal all of our diseases. Many times I have heard verse 1 sung and followed by "He has done great things." These Hebrew scholars continue verifying the intent of this Psalm by saying, "This pensive song, so powerful in its tone, has an Aramaic colouring …"[4]

No New Testament writer connects Psalm 103:3 with guaranteed healing by claiming it, declaring it, or confessing it as "already done at the cross" in reference to Christ's atonement. Biblical confirmation from Leviticus 13-14 has shown that physical healing did not come through the blood of animal sacrifices. Mr. Bosworth did not teach the truth about healing in Leviticus 13-14. Next, we will look at how Matthew understood Isaiah 53:4, and he was taught by Jesus.

Matthew 8:17 Helps Discern Isaiah 53:4

There are two Hebrew words in Isaiah 53:4 that need explanation so people cannot be deceived into believing this verse guarantees "atonement healing" for all sickness and disease for Christians. The two italicized words will be our focus for understanding this passage.

> Surely He hath *borne* our griefs, and *carried* our sorrows: yet we did esteem Him stricken, smitten of God, and afflicted.

To convince people that physical healing comes through Christ's atonement, faith healers preach that "Since the same Hebrew verbs *nâsâ* (bear, carry away, take away [5]) and *câbal* (bear, carry, strong to labor [6]) are found in verses 4, 11, and 12, then the same meaning must be applied in these verses; namely, that of atonement sin-bearing and atonement sickness-bearing. This being the case, we are guaranteed both forgiveness and physical healing."

Are these two Hebrew words tied to Christ's work on the cross, what He did during His ministry, or both? Was Isaiah teaching that those who received Messiah's forgiveness were also *guaranteed* physical healing through the atonement during their lifetime? Or is he also describing certain things about the Messiah so people will know His identity? Could Isaiah 53:4 be a "dual prophecy," a prophecy that occurs during Christ's ministry, *and* when He dies on the cross?

When reading the information in Isaiah 52:15-53:12, it is clear that these verses contain characteristics and descriptions pointing to the Messiah's identity, His ministry, and what His atoning death will accomplish. Therefore, if the *same* Hebrew words are used in different verses, we must discern the writer's communication intent in each verse. When studying a specific word in a verse, the words before and after the word being studied should also be considered.

The context in Isaiah 53:11-12 refers to the Messiah as our Intercessor Who will make atonement and bear our sins and iniquities. In verse 4, the words "smitten of God" refer to Jesus' time on the cross when the LORD put the iniquity of all upon Him (verse 6). The Hebrew word for "griefs" (*chŏlîy*) in verse 4 can also be translated "disease."[7] Since the words "borne" and "carried" in verse 4 describe Christ's atoning work, as does verse 5, does this automatically mean we are guaranteed both physical healing *and* spiritual healing?

The answer is "No," because Jesus taught the apostles to preach that *only* "repentance and remission of sins should be preached in His Name" (Luke 24:47). Jesus did not instruct His apostles to preach a Gospel of "repentance and the remission of sins and remission of all disease and sickness." When you read the various Gospel messages preached in *The Book of Acts*, you will *know* that not one message included guaranteed healing by believing in Christ's shed blood. The Gospel His disciples preached *guaranteed* forgiveness to any who sought God's forgiveness and believed in Jesus (Romans 10:9-10).

Though the words "borne" and "carried" in verse 4 describe what Christ took upon Himself (our griefs, sorrows, sickness) while making atonement for our sins, this does not mean He literally took all sickness and disease *into* His body, as He did all sin. Sickness, disease, and death came upon man because of sin. Therefore, the sin He bears in His body covers *all* the consequences of sin that will grieve mankind, including the various diseases and sicknesses that came into our world because of sin from the Garden of Eden.

If on the cross, Christ literally bears and takes into His body every disease and sickness in history then He will be mute, blind, and deaf. However, Jesus had vision and speech till death (John 19:26-30).

Though Isaiah 53:4 is connected with Christ's atonement, the physical healing benefits are separate from the spiritual healing benefits of verse 5.

Christ's atonement does *not* guarantee us heaven on earth throughout our life. It guarantees us heaven in heaven, *when* we get there. Until we get to heaven, we will have encounters with sickness, sorrow, and grief. Matthew 8 will teach us more about Isaiah 53:4.

Matthew 8:16 describes an evening when Jesus cast out demons and healed the sick, and we learn "That it might be fulfilled which was spoken by Isaiah the prophet, saying, Himself took our infirmities, and bare our sicknesses" (verse 17). This is a quote from Isaiah 53:4, and Matthew says this was fulfilled *during* Jesus' ministry *prior* to His blood atonement. Isaiah 53:4 is *also* prophetic to verify His Messianic ministry recorded in Matthew 8:17. Therefore, Isaiah 53:4 has "dual prophecy" implications with different teachings about His atonement and His earthly healing ministry.

Matthew refers to the healing work recorded in Isaiah 53:4 as taking place *during* the ministry of Christ when he writes verse 17. Yet, Isaiah's use of the Hebrew language implies that Isaiah 53:4 is connected to the atonement. Is this a contradiction between these two instruments chosen by God to pen different parts of the Bible? Or do we have a situation where the Holy Spirit put in Isaiah 53:4 both a temporal remedy for removing (taking away) *some* disease in a cursed world, and an eternal remedy for eliminating all disease forever *when* we reside in heaven?

Before this can be answered, we need to look at the way Matthew selected a critical word (bare/bear) in verse 17. The Greek word for "bare" or "bear" in verse 17 is *bastazō*. Here is how it's used:

> It is used with the meaning (a) to take up, as in picking up anything, stones, John 10:31; (b) to carry something, Matt 3:11; Mark 14:13 ... (c) to bear a burden, whether physically, as of the Cross, John 19:17, or metaphorically in respect of

sufferings endured in the cause of Christ, Luke 14:27; ... of sufferings borne on behalf of others, Matt. 8:17; Romans 15:1; Gal. 6:2.[8]

Inspired by God, Matthew uses *bastazō* because it does not carry the meaning of atonement in describing what Jesus did in verse 17. It is a word used to describe day-to-day healings. If he had wanted to tie the setting in verse 16 to the atonement in a way that it would teach guaranteed physical healing for all, Matthew would have used the Greek word *anapherō,* which has a definite atonement connection.

It is used twice of the Lord's propitiatory sacrifice, in His bearing sins on the Cross, Heb. 9:28 and I Peter 2:24.[9]

Matthew's choice of *bastazō* (sympathetic bearing) instead of *anapherō* (blood sacrificial bearing on the cross) was in obedience to what the Holy Spirit wanted taught in verse 17. All of Matthew 8:1-16 describes Christ's healing ministry and establishes His *identity*, not His atonement.

If the Holy Spirit had wanted Matthew to definitely teach guaranteed "atonement healing" in verse 17, this would have been an ideal place. He could have told Matthew to use *anapherō* instead of *bastazō* in verse 17. Then Matthew could have finished verse 17 by recording "and by His stripes we are healed" from Isaiah 53:5. Such a proclamation would have indicated atonement physical healing for all. Matthew did not do this when writing verse 17, because as an apostle he understood the difference between the atonement and the healing ministry of Jesus. Do you?

Some argue that verse 17 cannot be used to teach the identity of the Messiah. They say Jesus wanted to conceal His identity and quote these verses as proof: Matthew 12:15-16; Mark 3:11-12; 8:29-30. It is true that His identity was not meant to be exposed too early during His ministry, and there was a reason for this. Jesus had many prophecies to fulfill prior to His atonement. There is an appointed time for everything (Ecclesiastes 3:1), and for a period of time the multitudes of people were not to know Jesus of Nazareth was the Messiah. He had work to do for His Father (John 4:34) before He went to the cross.

Eventually Jesus wanted His apostles to know He was the Son of God, but they were to conceal His identity for a period of time (Matthew 16:13-20). Later, *all* were to know of Jesus and His salvation (Acts 4:12). Matthew 8:17 is written for teaching both the earthly healing ministry *and* the Messianic identity of Jesus as foretold in Isaiah 53:4.

It appears that Isaiah 53:4 is a "dual prophecy." 1) Jesus fulfilled part of it during His physical and spiritual healing ministry (Matthew 9:5-6) prior to His death on the cross. 2) The rest of it is fulfilled on the cross as foretold by Isaiah, bringing complete spiritual *and* physical healing "in heaven" to *all* who will receive Him as Lord and Savior (John 1:12; Romans 10:9-10).

After Christ's atonement, the Holy Spirit came at Pentecost with various gifts for the Body of Christ. He is one of the benefits of Christ's sacrificial death, resurrection, and ascension back to heaven (John 14:17, 26; 15:26-27; Acts 1:4-11). Since the Holy Spirit gives gifts of physical healing as He wills (1 Corinthians 12:9, 11) and *not* by our will, then healing is connected with Christ's atonement, but *not* guaranteed for all. You cannot claim your physical healing as already done. Anyone who seeks healing must pray to the LORD to find out "if" the Holy Spirit will bestow a gift of healing.

God wants us to trust in Him when seeking healing, rather than to blurt out a "faith confession" of already being healed. The LORD desires spiritual intimacy with His children. The sins of false teaching and false belief destroy spiritual intimacy with the Lord. Has your spiritual intimacy with the real Jesus been blocked because you have believed false faith teachings on healing?

Are Word of Faith Televangelists Misleading Millions?

Benny Hinn's atonement healing doctrine that Isaiah 53:4 and Matthew 8:16-17 provide healing for all was found to be unscriptural. And Fred Francis Bosworth's (1877-1958) false Levitical atonement healing doctrine combined with Matthew 8:16-17 was refuted. Don't allow any televangelists or any writings of deceased people persuade you to be deceived. Don't leave the truth about the real Jesus and His healing ministry for "another Jesus" healing ministry.

Endnotes:

1. Benny Hinn, *The Blood*, (Lake Mary, FL: Charisma House Publishing, 2006), pp. 198, 199.
2. F. F. Bosworth, *Christ the Healer*, (Grand Rapids, Michigan: Chosen Books, 2008), p. 30.
3. C. F. Keil and Franz Delitzsch, *Commentary on the Old Testament*, Volume 5, *Psalms, Fourth Book Of The Psalter* (Grand Rapids, Michigan: William B. Eerdmans Publishing Company, 1978), p. 118.
4. Ibid., p. 119.
5. James Strong, *Strong's Exhaustive Concordance of the Bible*, (Nashville, Tennessee: Abingdon Press, 1976), p. 80.
6. Ibid., p. 82.
7. Ibid., p. 39.
8. W. E. Vine, *An Expository Dictionary of New Testament Words*, (Old Tappan, New Jersey: Fleming Revell Company, 1966), pp. 100, 101.
9. Ibid., p. 101.

Chapter 16

1 Peter 2:24 Clarifies Isaiah 53:5

Advocates of "guaranteed atonement healing" constantly declare in their literature and messages that "By His stripes we are healed." This phrase is found in the last part of Isaiah 53:5 and also 1 Peter 2:24. International faith preachers emphasize that this phrase means we are *already* healed physically and spiritually. All we have to do is claim our healing by faith, as we claim our salvation by faith. If we have enough faith, we will be healed. They say our healing was *purchased* by Jesus with His shed blood when He died on the cross, while also forgiving our sins. Some call this verse "God's promise to heal."

Let's look at Isaiah 53:5 to search out the Holy Spirit's inspiration to the prophet Isaiah. I will italicize important words which guide us to how the Lord Jesus wants His followers to comprehend this verse.

> But He was wounded for our *transgressions*, He was bruised for our *iniquities*: the chastisement of *our peace* was upon Him; and with His stripes we are healed.

Our focus will be on the words, "transgressions," "iniquities," and "our peace." These words refer directly to our *spiritual* healing relationship with God, not our guarantee to receive *physical* healing through Messiah's atonement. Christ's purpose for being wounded, bruised, and chastised for us on the cross was to reconcile us through His forgiveness so we would have peace with His Father in heaven.

Still, Word of Faith believers say that the word "healed" signifies both spiritual and physical healing in this verse. They completely refuse to accept the obvious context of the italicized words which define the Holy Spirit context of how the word "healed" was inspired to Isaiah for our understanding.

The Hebrew word for "healed" in this passage is *râphâ*. It is used in many ways to convey the writer's specific intent. *Râphâ* can mean:

cure, (cause to) heal, physician, repair, make whole.[1]

This Hebrew word for healing is used in a variety of ways in the Old Testament. *Râphâ* is used to describe physical healing in Exodus 15:26; Numbers 12:13; 2 Kings 20:1-11; Psalm 103:3; healing of the land in 2 Chronicles 7:14; healing of water in 2 Kings 2:21-22, and spiritual healing in Psalm 41:4; 147:3; Isaiah 6:10; 53:5; Jeremiah 3:22; 15:18; Hosea 7:1, and 14:4.

The meaning of *râphâ* is not in question when studying Isaiah 53:5, for we know that it means to heal. It is the usage of *râphâ* by Isaiah, who was inspired by the Holy Spirit that is to be considered. Isaiah 53:5 says Jesus was wounded (pierced) for our transgressions and crushed (bruised) for our iniquities. This verse does not mention physical disease or sickness. It states that man is spiritually sick within, needs to have his sins forgiven, and by Christ's scourging we are healed, *so that we would have peace* (reconciliation) with God.

Isaiah 61:1 is a prophecy describing the Messiah's ministry and gives clarification to 53:5. It says:

The Spirit of the Lord God is upon Me; because the LORD hath anointed Me to preach good tidings unto the meek; He hath sent Me to bind up the brokenhearted, to proclaim liberty to the captives, and the opening of the prison to them that are bound.

Jesus reads this Messianic identity prophecy in Luke 4:18 and says, "He hath sent Me to heal the brokenhearted." Jesus does not say He was sent to heal all sickness and disease, though He did heal multitudes. But He also "withdrew" from multitudes (did not heal them) who wanted His healing (Luke 5:15-16). And He was selective when healing only one in a multitude who continually sought healing

(John 5:1-9), because He always did His Father's will (John 5:19-20). Scripture teaches it is *not* always God's will to heal everyone who wants to be healed, or believes they have healing faith.

Nowhere in the New Testament does it say Jesus was bruised, crushed, pierced, or wounded for our physical sicknesses and diseases. Paul writes in 1 Corinthians 15:3 "that Christ died for our sins according to the Scriptures." In Paul's numerous epistles, he never said Christians were *guaranteed* healing through the atonement of the Messiah Jesus. We can have assurance that when he talked with the apostles, who were taught by Jesus for at least three years, Paul knew how to teach the atoning work of the Lord Jesus (Galatians 1:11-12). New Testament authors never taught in their writings that Isaiah 53:5 guaranteed physical healing for all who receive Jesus as Lord.

Before the Holy Spirit came at Pentecost, Jesus said His apostles would receive power to be His witnesses (Acts 1:8). Jesus knew exactly what His atonement represented and how He wanted His followers to preach and teach it. Jesus did not tell them to preach that His death on the cross was to physically heal as many as received Him as Lord and Savior. He told them to preach repentance and remission of sins in His Name (Luke 24: 46-47). Read chapter 2 of Acts. Though Peter had apostolic healing power, he preached a message of "guaranteed forgiveness" (verses 36-40) as instructed by Jesus, not guaranteed forgiveness *and* healing.

When studying the repetitious content and Hebrew words referring to man's sin and rebellion in Isaiah 52:15-53:12 (describing the Messianic work on the cross), it is clear the message in verse 5 refers to *spiritual healing* that will reconcile man to God. Though physical healing will be a major part of Christ's ministry, it will *not* be guaranteed for all through His shed blood and death on the cross.

Consider this; if healing was guaranteed like salvation through the atonement for as many as believe, there would no need for the "gifts of healing" (1 Corinthians 12:9). The healing gifts were given as one of many functions of the Holy Spirit Who came at Pentecost. This gift is bestowed *by grace* proceeding from "the will of God" (verse 11), not man's will by claiming "By His stripes I am healed!" When writing to the Corinthians, Paul does *not* connect the gift of healing to the atonement as a guarantee for all who receive Jesus.

However, the following faith ministers teach that Isaiah 53:4-5, Matthew 8:17, and 1 Peter 2:24 provide evidence that a Christian's physical healing was purchased through Christ's atonement:

> Kenneth Copeland—*You Are Healed!* 1979, pp. 9-12.
> Kenneth Hagin—*Plead Your Case*, 1979, p. 28.
> John Hagee—*The Power of The Prophetic Blessing*, 2012, pp.159, 160.
> E. W. Kenyon & Don Gossett—*Speak Life*, 2013, p. 18.
> E. W. Kenyon—*What Happened from the Cross to the Throne*, 2010, pp. 108, 130.
> Joyce Meyer—*Be Healed in Jesus' Name*, 2000, pp. 16-19.
> T. L. Osborn—*Healing The Sick*, 1992, p. 117.
> Dodie Osteen—*If My Heart Could Talk, 2016*, p. 169.
> Rod Parsley—*At The Cross Where Healing Begins*, 2003, pp. 37-39.
> Frederick K. C. Price—*Is Healing for All?* 2015, pp. 120-121.
> Joseph Prince—*Healing Promises*, 2012, pp. 17-19.

Scriptural presentation from the last chapter and more Scripture from this chapter continually verify that their "healing for all through the shed blood of Christ" is not taught in the Bible.

Obvious Insight from 1 Peter 2:24

Many Word-Faith healers believe 1 Peter 2:24 means physical healing and does not mean spiritual healing. To discern the meaning of this verse, one must look back at verse 21 which refers to suffering and Christ's example for us to follow. Verse 22 says He "did no sin."

Verse 23 mentions that when Jesus suffered or was reviled, He did not respond improperly. Peter does not record anything in these three verses about physical healing. Yet, Word of Faith people teach that verse 24 guarantees physical healing, because it says "by whose stripes you were healed." But is this accurate?

Before Peter writes "by whose stripes you were healed" in verse 24, he writes that Jesus bare our sins in His body on the tree, that we might die to sin and live to righteousness. Peter does not record that "we might die to sickness and disease." Verse 25 refers to people as sheep who continually went astray, and have returned to the Shepherd of their souls. Verses surrounding verse 24 (verses 21-23, 25) do not talk about sickness and physical healing. The obvious context is spiritual healing, because those who have strayed from God have returned and *received forgiveness*. Have you strayed in deception?

Some false faith people say that the word "healed" in verse 24 also can mean physical healing so this verse refers to physical healing, not spiritual healing. The proper context of how Peter uses it, not our "faith opinion" determines the correct way God wants us to believe it. The Greek word for "healed" in verse 24 is *iaomai* and means:

> to heal, is used (a) of physical treatment 22 times; in Matt. 15:28, A. V., "made whole," R. V., "healed;" so in Acts 9:34; (b) figuratively, of spiritual healing, Matt. 13:15; John 12:40; Acts 28:27; Hebrews 12:13; 1 Peter 2:24; possibly, Jas. 5:16 includes both (a) and (b) ... Luke 4:18.[2]

Since the Greek word for "healed" *(iaomai)* in verse 24 can be used to convey spiritual or physical healing, we must carefully read the contextual use of *iaomai* to discern how the Holy Spirit wants us to understand its meaning. Peter's God-inspired use of *iaomai* in verse 24 establishes that he is teaching spiritual healing (forgiveness to live a righteous life), not physical healing.

The following list of Scriptures confirms Jesus came to redeem us and die *for the sins of the world*, not to heal all our diseases:

> Matthew 1:21; 26:28; John 1:29; Romans 3:25; 1 Corinthians 15:3-4; Galatians 1:4; Ephesians 1:7; 1 Timothy 1:15; Titus 2:14; Hebrews 1:3; 2:17; 7:27; 9:26, 28; 10:12; 1 Peter 3:18; 1 John 2:2; 4:10; Revelation 1:5.

If "healing for all" comes through the atonement as false faith people claim, then these verses just listed should contain explicit evidence to back their claims. However, *none* of these verses teach that Jesus gave His blood, and died to physically heal all Christians.

Their improper use of 1 Peter 2:24 is an ongoing and destructive way false faith healers isolate a verse, teach it wrong, and then it becomes a worldwide false doctrine. Their numerous false doctrines have caused an epidemic of spiritual sickness all over the world. Deliverance from deception is needed. Nowhere in *The Book of Acts* was 1 Peter 2:24 mentioned for physical healing when any Gospel message was preached. Jesus came to heal the broken-hearted (Isaiah 61:1; Luke 4:18).

Answer These Questions

1. 2 Peter 3:9 teaches God's foremost will is that none should perish, and all should repent and be saved. Is there a verse teaching God's foremost will is for all to be healed?

2. If we use Hebrews 13:8 to proclaim guaranteed healing because Jesus is "the same yesterday, today, and forever," then what about His healing of "only one man" when *many* were seeking healing in John 5:2-9? And He turned away from multitudes seeking healing in Luke 5:15-16. Jesus *did not* heal everyone who sought healing from Him. The context of Hebrews 13:8 doesn't teach guaranteed healing for all.

3. Some sickness/disease is demonic (Matthew 12:22). If Jesus bore *all* diseases in His body while on the cross, as some faith ministers teach, then according to *their* teachings Jesus was demon-possessed during His atonement, because some demons that cause disease indwell the person. Thus, false faith people have a demon-indwelled savior on the cross who was defeated by Satan, instead of the sinless Holy Son of God Who defeated Satan on the cross (Colossians 2:14-15). Satan must be very happy about *their* false teaching that makes it look like his demons were on the flesh of Jesus and inside Jesus during His time on the cross. Do you now have a better picture of how certain false faith people view the sacrifice of the Lord Jesus? They give the devil improper recognition with *their* false atonement teaching.

4. Mark 16:18 and James 5:14-16 mention healing, but no evidence is listed to support *guaranteed* healing through the atonement for all. Is God's Word trying to tell us the obvious?

5. Does the Covenant in Romans 11:26-27 say the Deliverer will come from Zion, remove ungodliness from Jacob, take away their sins, *and* take away all disease and poverty?

6. Did Jesus teach His atonement guaranteed that it is God's will for all Christians to be healed and walk in "Divine" health?

From this Scriptural study on the Messiah's atonement, we learned that physical healing is a gift from the Holy Spirit Who came *after* Christ's atonement and ascension (Acts 1:4-8; 2:1-4). Though the New Covenant Holy Spirit "gifts of healing" are linked with Christ's atonement benefits, healing is *not* guaranteed for all in the same way that forgiveness is guaranteed for all who repent of their sins. Holy Spirit "gifts of healing" occur as He wills (1 Corinthians 12:9, 11), not as man wills. Therefore, anyone who teaches you are "already" healed physically because of Christ's atonement is not telling the truth, and endorses a "false healing Jesus."

Also, when seeking healing, the word "if" does not mean you lack faith to receive your healing. It means in accordance with God's will (1 John 5:14). In Matthew 8:2, a leper comes to Jesus and says "Lord, if Thou wilt, Thou canst make me clean." Jesus does not scold the person for lack of faith because of using the word "if." Jesus healed the leper, because it was God's will at that time.

Correction is needed for another false faith healing teaching that claims, "You can command yourself to be healed because of Isaiah 53:5. Claim your healing and speak to your area of sickness." If Christians do this, they intercede for Jesus and command the Holy Spirit to obey them and heal the sickness. Who is Lord of healing, you or Jesus? So where is this teaching found? Could it be from the occult?

Our answer is found in a book by Ann Fisher titled *Omni-Cosmics: Miracle Power Beyond the Subconscious*. She is a nationally recognized psychic and metaphysician. She understands occult power.

> You have the power to command yourself to be healed by auto-suggestion or concentration. Your mind directs the psychic energy, but without this mental power there would be no psychic or occult power.[3]

This "Command yourself to be healed" teaching is used in the occult where auto-suggestion (speaking to yourself, commanding the area to be healed) directs the power of healing. This is not Holy Spirit healing, because we don't tell the Holy Spirit what to do and when to do it. Partnering with this occult teaching, pastor Joel Osteen says:

> If you have health problems, instead of begging God to heal you, you need to declare to that sickness, "Sickness, you have

no right in my body. I'm a child of the Most High God. You are not welcome here. And I'm not asking you to leave.... No, I'm commanding you to leave my body."[4]

More than once, Daystar Christian Network has called Joel Osteen "The most watched influential figure in America." Do his millions of viewers worldwide realize, and those who have purchased his books, that he doesn't teach healing according to the Scriptures? A way to discern false teachers is their ability to make up stuff about what they teach, with no Scripture in context as proof.

Jesus never taught that Christians should speak healing to their bodies. Joel Osteen needs to read Philippians 2:25-29, 1 Timothy 5:23, and 2 Timothy 4:20 in order to learn God's way of healing, or *not* healing. The apostle Paul did not tell any of the sick mentioned in the last sentence that they should/could command the sickness to leave their body. Paul had a true apostolic healing ministry with signs and wonders (2 Corinthians 12:12), and he knew the truth about healing.

Pastor Joel Osteen oversees a huge congregation. He has the opportunity and the obligation to the Lord Jesus to Shepherd properly (1 Peter 5:1-4) a flock of many for the glory of God. Sound doctrine is his obligation. Please pray for his repentance.

If anyone tells you that Christians can use this "verbal command" for personal healing, you now know that it was not the Lord Jesus Who spoke to them. Jesus does not promote occult healing. Yet, some who *claim* to be Christian faith healers are teaching healing with an occult connection. Among faith healing ministries, I have continued to find common doctrinal errors; they preach false doctrine on healing, preach "another Jesus," and a false prosperity gospel. Any false gospel is a sin-filled gospel of bad news, *not* a sin-free Gospel of good news.

We should also be concerned for the Jews who are receiving salvation messages about this false "healing for all" atonement, an atonement the true Messiah Jesus did not preach. The Jewish people have suffered immensely at various times in history. They don't need to hear about a *counterfeit Messiah* and a false atonement.

Presenting another Yeshua (Jesus) to the Jews, who is *not* their long-awaited Savior from the God of Abraham, Isaac, and Jacob, is blasphemous deception! The Worldwide Faith Movement has this huge sin (guaranteed atonement healing) in large print on *their* lengthy false teaching "rap sheet." They must honor the real Jesus Who "took the rap" for their sins by serving *their* sinful time on the cross to provide forgiveness; they must honor Him with repentance!

Christ has redeemed us from the eternal death penalty of sin through His atonement, but the *total effect* of our redemption from sin has not yet manifested. Presently, we rejoice in the forgiveness of our sins while the inward man is being renewed day by day (2 Corinthians 4:16). Romans 8:23 tells us we groan within ourselves, waiting for our adoption as sons, the redemption of our body.

In the future, Christ's atonement will remove and annul every curse, all pain, all sickness, and all suffering (Revelation 21:1-5; 22:1-5) that entered through one man's sin (Romans 5:12-19). Then we can enjoy our "guaranteed" eternal healing provision through the Lord's atonement. Forever, we will be with the Lord and His constant love.

Endnotes:

1. James Strong, *Strong's Exhaustive Concordance of the Bible*, (Nashville, Tennessee: Abingdon Press, 1976), p. 110.

2. W. E. Vine, *An Expository Dictionary of New Testament Words*, (Old Tappan, New Jersey: Fleming Revell Company, 1966), Vol. II, E-Li, p. 203.

3. Ann Fisher, *Omni—Cosmics: Miracle Power Beyond the Subconscious*, (West Nyack, New York: Parker Publishing Company, 1979), p. 52.

4. Joel Osteen, *I Declare 31 Promises to Speak Over Your Life* (New York, NY: FaithWords, 2013), p. 162.

Chapter 17

Discerning Supernatural Healing Power

We will now take a Scriptural look at a very controversial area; namely, that physical healings have occurred in Word of Faith gatherings. Specifically, what is the "supernatural" source (or sources) of power that produces healing among people in the Worldwide Faith Movement? Is it from the LORD, from evil healing spirits, or both sources? These are the choices we have, because Scripture confirms obvious healing activity from only two miraculous sources. Those two sources will now be shown.

There is no need to present the abundance of Gospel events where Jesus healed and did miracles through the power of the Holy Spirit. Messiah's miraculous lifestyle is foretold in the Old Testament, and recorded in the New Testament. Our focus will be on Scripture which helps us to see that demonic spirits can also perform the miraculous in the presence of God's servants, as well as those who become deceived and follow foreign gods.

The LORD did mighty signs and wonders when preparing to bring His people out of Egypt (Exodus 7-12). Pharaoh's magicians (sorcerers) duplicated some of the miracles God did through Moses and Aaron (Exodus 7:10-12, 20-22; 8:6-7). Finally, Pharaoh let God's people go. This sorcery/magic duplication of God's miracles (signs and wonders) verifies that Satan has the power to counterfeit some works of the Holy Spirit. The evil one has the supernatural power to "manifest matter and change the physical elements of nature."

At times people argue about how demons got their supernatural power, and overlook the fact that demonic influence is global. (Ephesians 2:2; 1 John 5:19). The important concern when discussing this topic is that demons do have spiritual power to deceive, and to do signs and wonders that look like the power of the Holy Spirit. As the

Hebrews traveled by God's guidance, the Law was given to Moses over a period of time. In Deuteronomy 13:1-4, Moses warns the people about false signs and wonders that could occur in their midst. Moses says these false supernatural events are to *test* God's people to see if they would "go after other gods" and "serve them." These verses teach that the LORD God gives His people free will to choose between demonic signs and wonders, or remain dedicated to Him.

Jeremiah 44:15-19 confirms that when God's people departed from His Law and worshipped the queen of heaven, demon activity *provided* for their needs, and these demon worshippers "saw no evil" (verse 17). This teaches us Satan will bestow counterfeit material blessings to those who once followed the true God, and then choose to follow other gods. The signs of deception for these in the time of Jeremiah were "victuals" and protection from evil.

In Matthew 12:22-24, the Pharisees accuse Jesus of doing His miraculous works by the power of Beelzebub, the prince of the devils. They knew of the warning in Deuteronomy 13:1-4 about signs and wonders of deception. Though they did not believe Jesus was the Messiah, they did not question that His miraculous works were for real. The rejection of Jesus' miraculous works, as from the Holy Spirit, shows that some of the Pharisees believed demonic power could do healings (Mark 3:1-6) and cast out demons (Mark 1:21-27) in their synagogues where the Scripture was opened and taught.

We will now take a detailed look at the possibility of demonic spirits healing Christians. Then we will look at ways Holy Spirit healings *could* be happening in the false Faith Movement.

Can Demonic Spirits Heal Christians?

This is a hotly debated question, but it *must* be answered when addressing the numerous miraculous physical healing claims for decades that continue to come from the various worldwide faith healing ministries. We cannot deny that some people have been healed while attending Word-Faith conferences when prayer is offered for the many seeking healing from sickness and extreme pain.

In presenting the *possibility* of demonic power healing Christians, it must be stated that I am not saying that demons must indwell (be inside) Christians in order to heal them. When Jesus healed the multitudes, there is no Scripture telling us all the healed *were indwelled* with the Holy Spirit when and after they were healed. The Holy Spirit came at Pentecost to indwell believers (Romans 8:9, 11) after Jesus went back to heaven (John 14:16-17, 26; 15:26; 16:7). We need to look at the power of demonic healing spirits to see if they can heal the flesh without indwelling, or possessing the person.

Common arguments and Scriptures used that supposedly teach a demon cannot heal a Christian will now be presented:

1. The belief that being "sealed by the Holy Spirit" (Ephesians 1:13; 4:30) to teach no demonic power can enter a Christian is wrong. These verses do not teach this. They teach about salvation and redemption. Demon activity is not the issue before or after these verses. The fiery darts (Satan's spiritual verbal assault) mentioned in Ephesians 6:16 indicate his spiritual words can enter our minds if we allow it. Examples confirming this are found in Matthew 16:21-23, Luke 22:31, and Acts 5:1-11, where Peter states that Ananias and Sapphira allowed Satanic words of deception to fill their hearts. They were not demon-indwelled, but they agreed with the evil one and chose to receive Satan's spiritual power (words of deception) into their hearts. The Holy Spirit seal mentioned in Ephesians 1:13; 4:30 doesn't promise a believer immunity against demonic influence.

2. Some use 1 Corinthians 3:16 and 6:19 (we are the temple of God) to teach, "Since the Spirit of God dwells in you, no

demon activity can enter you, because God and Satan cannot be in the same place (your body)." These two verses do not guarantee all Christians ongoing demonic immunity. The context of complete protection from the fiery darts that can enter the mind and heart, if permitted, is not recorded in these verses. Our body is the temple of the Holy Spirit, and if we abuse and neglect it we get sick. Bacterial and viral infections can invade the body, and they don't have the intelligence of a demon that can speak invasive thoughts which enter the mind and cause spiritual sickness, leading to sin.

3. Some say the phrase in 1 John 5:18, "and the wicked one toucheth him not" means Satan can't touch us in any spiritual or physical way. Look at the entire verse. It is true, when you abstain from sin, you keep yourself protected from the wicked one. But Christians who entertain demonic verbal influence aren't keeping themselves protected. This is what we are dealing with in the false doctrine of the Worldwide Faith Movement. False doctrine from seducing spirits (1 Timothy 4:1) provides entry for evil spirit influence to receptive minds. Then demonic spiritual influence, as recorded in Acts 5:1-11, is manifested in one's new/false belief.

Though the LORD fills the heavens and the earth (Jeremiah 23:24), and His presence is in Hades (Psalm 139:7-8), He permits demonic spirits to roam the earth and tempt all humanity (Luke 4:1-11), and He allows demons in His presence (Job 1:6-12; 2:1).

Scriptural information revealing how demonic spiritual influence can enter a Christian's mind has been shown. Our next step is to show how healing demons will heal anyone. Earlier it was shown in Exodus 7:10-8:7 that demons can do miracles by changing the physical elements of nature. Previous Scripture showed demonic darts can change a believer's spiritual pattern of thinking, but is it also possible that demonic healing spirits can heal diseases and change/restore flesh in a miraculous way similar to a Holy Spirit healing? To answer this question, we will see what Scripture discloses about angels being involved with miraculous healings. Follow patiently for a few pages.

Does God Heal Through Holy Angels?

John 5:2-9 records a time where Jesus selects only one person to heal among "a great multitude" who were seeking healing from God. Verse 4 says "an angel went down at a certain season into the pool and troubled the water," and whoever stepped in was healed of their disease (verse 4). Far too many people have misunderstood this verse by using it to teach that God's Holy angels do physical healing.

This setting teaches that the angel *only* stirs/troubles the water. Nowhere in verse 4 does it say the angel did the healing. In the New Covenant, healing is given "by gifts of the Holy Spirit" (1 Corinthians 12:9, 11), *not* by gifts of healing angels. Jesus never taught His disciples to pray to, call upon, or believe in angels for healing. Despite John's easy to understand historical account, there are well-known faith teachers who reject this truth and teach God uses angels for healing:

> Imagine that your answer is on the way. God has already dispatched the angel with your healing.[1] (Joel Osteen).

> There are some people who have not been released from old trials yet because they will not allow God to heal them through the angels of ministry He has chosen to use.[2] (T. D. Jakes).

God "has chosen to use" His Son He sent to bind up and heal the broken-hearted (Psalm 147:3; Isaiah 61:1; Luke 4:18). The LORD is our Healer. His holy angels are His ministering servants (Psalm

103:20-21; Hebrews 1:14; 1 Peter 3:22), but holy angels do *not* minister physical healings. They watch their LORD do the healing and give Him praise (Psalm 148:2).

Our attention will now focus on a man who traveled the world with his healing ministry. Many faith healers hold him in high esteem because of his healing ministry. His doctrinal beliefs about the LORD, and whom he attributes his physical healing power to will surface in the buoyancy of truth.

William Branham's Healing Angel

William Branham (1909-1965) has been touted as a man with a genuine healing ministry. Forthcoming facts will confirm that his healing ministry didn't line up with a God-given Holy Spirit healing ministry. There is no point in denying that some people were healed through him as he traveled the world. Our focus will be on discerning the power that was used by Mr. Branham when healing the sick.

In his book, *Wandering Stars*, Keith Gibson documents vital facts exposing William Branham's healing ministry. Pastor Gibson reveals this information found in Robert Liardon's book, *God's Generals*:

> He taught that the doctrine of the Trinity was a doctrine of demons and that anyone baptized in the Trinitarian formula went into darkness. (Look at Matthew 28:19 for God's truth).

> He denied hell was eternal. (Eternal, everlasting, or day and night forever means a long time. Read Matthew 25:41 and Revelation 14:9-11; 20:10-15. In denying that hell is eternal or ongoing, Mr. Branham rejects the words of truth from Jesus).

> He taught that all disease was demonic. (Chapter 3 refuted the false belief that all disease is demonic).

He prophesied the destruction of the United States would begin in 1977. (We are still here decades later).

He taught that healings could be lost if a person quit believing.[3] (Not one verse about Jesus or apostolic healing teaches that Holy Spirit healings can be lost. Does a person have to believe till death, or they lose their healing? This is a weird and evil teaching).

By rejecting Scriptural teachings on baptism, hell, disease, and losing your healing, William Branham certainly proved himself to *not* be a true prophet from God. The LORD'S prophets honor His Word by teaching it in proper context. True prophets never rejected God's Word in any way or gave it a new meaning. Next, the source of the healing power of William Branham will be exposed.

When you have sufficient knowledge of William Branham's background, it is evident that unusual events occurred from his birth throughout his life; events that quickly cause one to question his life before and during his healing ministry years. These supernatural manifestations are, at times, bizarre. Here are some from a 3 page article I found online titled, *A Brief Biography of the Life of William Branham*.[4]

Right after he was born, a light, almost like a star, flew into the room and startled his parents.... The strange light circled the room several times, then stopped over the bed hovering over the new mother and child. Then as quickly as it had come in, the fireball left, whirling up past the rafters and out through the roof.

However, the most supernatural event that would affect William Branham happened when he was seven years old. He noticed a whirlwind in a tree. As he watched, a voice suddenly boomed from the tree saying, "*Don't ever drink, or smoke, or defile your body in any way. There will be work for you to do when you get older. "*

From then on, he would sometimes feel a presence or see visions of things that would terrify him. However, he did not think about God until he was fourteen.

One day he decided to tack a letter to a tree. He then went into the barn and prayed sincerely from his heart. When he opened his eyes he saw floating in front of him, a brilliant amber light, forming a perfect cross in the air. There, in that barn, he accepted the Lord Jesus Christ.

Meanwhile, the visions continued.... Desperation finally drove him to seek God in the wilderness, where he came face to face with a supernatural Being. This supernatural being, the angel of the Lord, gave him a commission from God to take the gift of Divine healing to the people of the world.

None of this supernatural spiritual activity that happened in Mr. Branham's life proves all or any of these events are from the LORD. Occult spirits have the supernatural ability to do these manifestations. Strange lights, fireballs, voices speaking out of the air, or by an object, whirlwinds (Job 1:19), a presence you sense, visions of terror, and a light shaped in the form of a cross in the air can manifest in occult activity (Matthew 24:24; Revelation 13:13-14).

Also, when the apostles received healing power (authority), they got it from Jesus, not an angel (Matthew 10:1; Luke 9:1-2). And Paul never said he received his true apostolic signs and wonders ministry from an angel (2 Corinthians 12:12; Galatians 1:11-12).

William Branham "claimed that all of his healings were done by his angel who always stood on his right side. For this reason, he always had people stand by his right side so they would get a double blessing."[5] When questioned, he attributed his miracles to this angel and not to God. From his own mouth, Mr. Branham said he did not have a Holy Spirit healing ministry.

In his book, *The Purpose of Temptation*, Bob Mumford relates a story in which a Christian went to pray and fast for three days in a hotel. On the third day, this Christian sensed what he thought was God's presence in the room. Before him stood a man, the most beautiful person he had ever seen, surrounded by an aura of light, and the desire to worship this person was strong. The person spoke to him and said, "If you worship me, I will give you a powerful healing ministry. All the world will know you!"[6]

The man was tempted, but deep within himself he heard the Name of Jesus. As he spoke it, the person vanished. A demonic spirit was willing to bless a Christian with a powerful healing ministry *if* the Christian would worship him. The demonic spirit was going to heal Christians through this man. This incident shows a demon was willing to empower a Christian with a healing ministry that resembles the Lord Jesus' healing power. One purpose was to be worshipped. Another purpose was to gain an influential stronghold in the person's life that would extend demonic healings to any in the Body of Christ who would let a healer with demonic power touch them, or pray for them.

This example of a demon offering a powerful healing ministry to a Christian is of great concern. If this man had said "Yes" to this deception, God alone knows how many Christians or secular people worldwide would have received healing and influence from a demon. And at this time, the LORD *knows* how many "false faith teachers with healing ministries" are empowered by demonic healing spirits.

A deceased friend of mine was a witch for many years. Late in life, with her years running short, she became a Christian. While practicing witchcraft, she used a powerful demonic healing spirit that did some amazing, quick healings. When she was a massage therapist, a hunchback came to her business for a massage. As he removed his shirt, she noticed how contorted his back was. This is what she said to the man: "Hey mister, do you want me to take that hump out of your back?" He responded in a sarcastic way and said, "Yeah. Sure lady. You can do that for me."

She went to another room and came back with her witchcraft healing oil. Then she poured some at the base of his neck and traced the oil with her finger down his entire spinal column. As she was doing this, she spoke "words of healing." When she finished her finger trail on the entire spine from neck to lower back, his spine began to straighten out. In less than thirty seconds his entire back was straightened. He looked up at her and said, "What are you?" She responded, "You know what I am." He was scared, picked up his clothes, and ran out of her office.

Another example of the healing power her demonic spirit had was displayed when a neighbor was working on her carburetor. The manifold was quite hot because she had been driving the car earlier. His hand slipped and his palm landed on the hot manifold. He let out a yell with intense pain. When she looked at his palm, the skin was burned deep and flesh had peeled away.

She told him she would go into the house and get some oil to soothe the pain. She came back with her vial of demonic blessed oil and asked him to open his hand so she could put some oil on it. When he did this, she poured the oil into his palm and rubbed it lightly. In a few seconds his burned tissue was replaced with new tissue. He was so scared he ran back to his house without his tools. Later he got them back.

According to this former witch, these two *demonic miraculous* healings, "when manifested," did not produce an evil presence. Her demonic healing spirit did not have to enter the person's body to heal. The power to heal emanated from its functioning presence and healing occurred, as the evil spirit stood beside her. This same counterfeit healing power has freedom to intermingle with false healers.

Christians need to realize that Eve detected no evil presence when the serpent talked to her and deceived her in the sin-free Garden of Eden. Therefore, when false healers are backed by demonic healing spirits, you cannot say the presence, if not unpleasant, is from the Holy Spirit. Satan's false apostles and false healers counterfeit signs and wonders (2 Corinthians 11:13-15).

The answer to the question, "Can a Christian receive healing from a demon?" will now be answered. Did *some* people get healed in William Branham's ministry by an angel? Yes. Can we say *all* the multitudes who attended his meetings were not Christians, and that is why they got healed? No. Many Christians attended his meetings.

William Branham denied the Godhead (Romans 1:20; Colossians 2:9), known as the Father, Son, and Holy Spirit Trinity. This means he denied the eternal, everlasting Deity of Messiah Jesus (Micah 5:2; John 1:1-3), as well as the eternal Holy Spirit (Hebrews 9:14). When tested by Scripture, his healing angel was *not* a Holy Spirit healing angel. From Acts 5:1-11, we know demonic influence that is accepted can reach the heart and change a person's mind. No verse teaches that a demon will not heal the flesh of a Christian, if given the chance.

Demonic healing spirit power does not have to indwell the person to heal. Thus, Christians seeking healing from a minister who is using demonic healing power open themselves up to the possibility of a demonic healing. Satan is a master counterfeiter (Matthew 24:24).

Does the Holy Spirit Still Heal Physically?

Reasons to consider the possibility of the Holy Spirit healing in the midst of false Word of Faith doctrine are:

1. God has given "gifts of healing" to certain people and *when* the LORD wants to use them for healing, He will. It is possible God has gifted Christians involved with the Faith Movement (those not entrenched with false doctrine) to

minister the "gift of healing" occasionally, *because* they don't preach "another Jesus." You might object to this because of the vast doctrinal sin in the false Faith Movement, but we must remember that even Judas Iscariot, who *betrayed* Jesus, had a healing ministry from God (Matthew 10:1-9). For *a time* Judas preached the truth (no evidence is found in the Gospels proving Judas preached a false Jesus) about Jesus, and healed with the other apostles. Then he betrayed the Lord for money. The "Jesus guarantees health and wealth" faith teachers have betrayed the Lord also. Their *betrayal* is in distorting the true identity of Jesus and emphasizing a different atonement for financial gain. If a person is truly gifted to preach, then using the Name of Jesus for monetary gain should not be connected with the God-given gifts of healing (Matthew 10: 9-10). Yet, this monetary guideline is neglected throughout the global false faith healing ministries. If "the gift of healing" is from the LORD, no false doctrine about Jesus and His atonement should come out of the mouth of the person who ministers "the gift of healing." Don't ever let anyone who preaches lies about Jesus and His atonement lay hands on you to pray for your healing. Why? Because if false doctrine people have demon activity working in or around them, you could receive *their* demonic influence and it will ensnare you, and lead you into consistent deception. Jesus, the apostles, and prophets laid the Church foundation (Ephesians 2:20). The foundation was not laid in false healings, false prophecies, or false doctrine. Such elements too often describe the many false faith healing ministries around the world.

2. God could honor individual or united faith in an audience *when* healing, in line with Scripture, is being preached. Therefore, He heals not only because of the preacher's

message, but also in response to the effectual fervent prayer from those in the crowd.

3. Demonic spirits are doing some of the healings. This would explain why healing recipients say they lost their healing. No verse teaches that a true healing from the Holy Spirit, Who worked through Jesus and the apostles, was ever "lost" due to lack of faith. When people preach, teach, and hold fast to "another gospel" (2 Corinthians 11:3-4) that falsifies Jesus (declaring He guarantees health and wealth for all through His blood, and teach He was beaten up by the devil and demons in hell for three days, because His shed blood on the cross *was not good enough* to forgive our sins) then healing demons could have access to their homes, churches, Bible studies, conferences, and healing seminars to counterfeit signs, wonders, and healings.

For those who wonder why demons would heal Christians, the answer is clear. If demonic healing spirits are allowed to heal in the Body of Christ, they will have the freedom to deceive people into believing the LORD has healed them. Then those who have received healing will spread false doctrine on healing, "another Jesus," a false gospel, and doctrinal deception with demonic assistance will increase worldwide. The constant demonic assault Paul cites in Ephesians 6:10-18 alerts us to stand firm against *all* wiles of deception.

Worldwide repentance from many preachers and authors of false healing doctrines is a must! However, some will never repent, but will remain snared by the devil to do his will (2 Timothy 2:25-26). Their success is backed by the pride of life, worldwide fame, and excessive prosperity. They look at what they have on the outside, rather than who they really are on the inside. Such an attitude will continue to blind their eyes to the truth and sear their conscience from accepting and preaching the true Gospel (2 Corinthians 4:3-4). They have their own definition of the Christian faith, but it's not "the faith" that the Lord Jesus taught.

When Jesus returns, will *you* be filled with His righteousness and true faith concerning sound doctrine on Holy Spirit healing, or filled with false faith concerning healing? (Luke 18:8). Remain free by knowing the truth, living the truth (John 8:31-32), and remaining in "the doctrine of Christ" (2 John 9).

Endnotes:

1. Joel Osteen, *The Power of I AM* (New York, New York: FaithWords, 2015), p. 22.
2. T. D. Jakes, *God Longs To Heal You* (Shippensburg, PA: Destiny Image Publishers, Inc., 1995), p. 164.
3. Keith Gibson, *Wandering Stars* (Birmingham, Alabama: Solid Ground Christian Books, 2011), pp. 280-281.
4. *A Brief Biography of the Life of William Branham.* Find this at: www.livingwordbroadcast.org/LWBPublications/WilliamBranham
5. Quoted from *Wandering Stars* by Keith Gibson. Roberts Liardon, *God's Generals* (Laguna Hills, California: Robert's Liardon Publishing, 1996), chapter 10, p. 309. "William Branham, A Man of Notable Signs and Wonders."
6. Bob Mumford, *The Purpose of Temptation* (Old Tappan, New Jersey: Fleming H. Revell, 1973), pp. 111, 112.

Chapter 18

The Cost of Accepting a False Gospel

The title of this chapter should be of great concern for anyone who wants assurance of Christ's forgiveness and eternal life in heaven. We will look at Scripture that clearly shows *exactly* the content of the only true Gospel Jesus directed His apostles and followers to teach. It is imperative for "those who claim to be Christians" to understand the overall consequences which arise from preaching, serving, and worshipping "another Jesus," and promoting "another gospel." Luke 24:46-47 proclaims the *only* Gospel of salvation Jesus ever told His disciples to preach:

> And He said unto them, "Thus it is written, and thus it behoved Christ to suffer, and to rise from the dead the third day: And that repentance and remission of sins should be preached in His Name among all nations, beginning at Jerusalem."

There is no acceptable way to break down the Greek word structure in these two verses and say it teaches the Gospel of Jesus guarantees forgiveness, physical healing, and financial prosperity. Throughout *The Acts of the Apostles*, Christ's disciples obeyed His Luke 24:46-47 instructions, and *never* included "By His stripes we are physically healed" in any of their messages.

Furthermore, when instructing His disciples on how to preach His Gospel, Jesus did not tie in "the curse of the Law" for guaranteed health and wealth for all. When Paul was called to preach the Gospel to honor the Lord Jesus, he preached it as recorded in 1 Corinthians 15:1-4. As a devout Jew (Philippians 3:5), he knew the Law well and taught when the Messiah redeemed us from the curse of the Law, we were justified through faith (Galatians 3:8, 13-14). Paul does not teach we were also assured health and wealth when we were justified.

Paul received God's true Gospel from Jesus by direct revelation (Galatians 1:11-12). In defense of its meaning, he reminded the church at Corinth to beware of any false gospels in 2 Corinthians 11:4. He directs their attention to those who preach "another Jesus," because it transforms the false message into "another gospel." When "another gospel" is preached, it sets itself *against* the true Gospel taught by Jesus and His apostles. This produces spiritual havoc and rejection of the true Gospel, as the false "threefold redemption gospel" has done.

When people teach "another Jesus," the false teaching brings "another spirit" and a false gospel with it, which is a non-saving false Jesus gospel. Therefore, the spiritual source/influence that endorses the false gospel *cannot* be the Holy Spirit, because He is the Spirit of truth (John 15:26). The apostle Paul alerts us that this deceptive spiritual influence is from those who don't have the truth about the real Jesus and His Gospel.

After he warns the Corinthian Church about those who teach a false Jesus and "another gospel" in verse 4, Paul continues on to verses 13-15. He writes that "Satan himself is transformed into an angel of light" (verse 14). The word "transformed" describes graphically what Satan's deceitful workers are like. As deceptive ministers they talk about Scripture, are involved with churches and act like Christians, but they "disguise the truth" by preaching "another Jesus" and a "different gospel." The test to reveal if they really were Christians (followers of the real Jesus) is whether they preached the true Gospel Paul preached (1 Corinthians 15:3-4).

Verses 13-15 are very bad news for any who preach or teach "another Jesus" because their "end shall be according to their works" (verse 15). These verses are not Paul's only warning to those who preach "another gospel." In Galatians 1:6, Paul expresses his disappointment that the Galatian Christians are removing themselves from the *only* Gospel Jesus will accept, and deserting Christ for "another gospel," a gospel he did not preach. We will look at verses 8 and 9 to see what the LORD told Paul to write about those who preach a gospel contrary to the true Gospel.

> But though we, or an angel from heaven, preach any other gospel unto you than that which we have preached unto you, let him be accursed. As we said before, so say I now again. If any man preach any other gospel unto you than that ye have received, let him be accursed.

The Greek word for "accursed" is *anathema,* and Paul uses it twice to warn all to the importance of the *only* Gospel Jesus will accept. The LORD inspires Paul to use this very harsh word of judgment on any who preach a gospel contrary to, or other than the original true Gospel Paul had taught the Galatians. The use of the word "any" means Paul is covering "any" false gospels that will ever be preached in the future. Concerning "anathema" Vine's *Expository Dictionary* gives this definition:

> In Gal. 1:8, 9, the Apostle declares in the strongest manner that the Gospel he preached was the one and only way of salvation, and that to preach another was to nullify the Death of Christ.[1]

Paul is inspired to let the Galatians and the rest of the world know that only one Gospel is acceptable to God. Embracing "another Jesus" gospel *nullifies* the death of Christ for one's sins. The false "threefold redemption gospel" that some cling to is unacceptable to God, because it teaches Jesus died to forgive our sins, guarantee healing, and guarantee abundant prosperity to all who believe in it.

According to these Scriptures (Galatians 1:6-9; 2 Corinthians 4:3-4; 11:3-4, 13-15), trusting in "another Jesus" and "another gospel" is placing faith in deception. Also, keep in mind Philippians 1:15-18 records that Paul says there are those who preach Christ with improper motives, but he is thankful that the true Christ is being preached. And Paul does not say they are preaching "another Jesus."

Christians are not called to ignore false teachings about Jesus that constitute a false gospel and keep people out of Heaven. We are called to defend the true faith (Jude 3-4). Misled faith preachers are not ashamed of the false gospel they *declare* around the globe. As true believers, we must not be ashamed to *defend* the true Gospel (Luke 24:45-47; Romans 1:16; 1 Corinthians 15:1-4).

The early Church did not open its doors to false teachers and invite them in for fellowship as if nothing was wrong. They did not say, "You can believe in Jesus your way and we will believe in Jesus our way." Those who were confronted and still taught false doctrine after repentance was urged were handled in this manner:

> Now I beseech you, brethren, mark them which cause divisions and offenses contrary to the doctrine which ye have learned; and avoid them (Romans 16:17).

This verse sets the standard we are to follow when we find those among us who teach false doctrine causing division and offenses. Those who cause factions *after* being warned prove their heretical attitude is sinful, and self-condemning (Titus 3:10-11). They are to be marked (exposed) as disrupters of the true faith and we are to avoid them. By avoiding them (not having fellowship with them), they are *marked* out among us and they will repent, or move on with their sin following them (Numbers 32:23). Do not allow them to participate in The Lord's Supper, choir, or teach any class.

With numerous false teachings exposed, the issue of heresy (false doctrine believed and taught) must be addressed. So how does one become a heretic? Vine's *Expository Dictionary of New Testament Words* provides the following description and mindset of those who become heretics *and* promote heresy:

HAIRESIS denotes (a) a choosing, choice (from *haireomai*, to choose); then, that which is chosen, and hence, an opinion, especially a self-willed opinion, which is substituted for submission to the power of truth, and leads to division and the formation of sects, Gal. 5:20; such erroneous opinions are frequently the outcome of personal preference or the prospect of advantage; see 2 Pet. 2:1, where "destructive" signifies leading to ruin.[2]

Read it again to fully comprehend what the mind of a heretic is like. Those who bring damnable heresies are mentioned in 2 Peter 2:1. They are called false prophets and false teachers. Such people reside and preach within the Word-Faith Movement, even *denying* the real Lord Who bought them, because they fulfill 2 Corinthians 11:4.

Three points of focus will show that "heresy" is an accurate label the Worldwide Faith Movement has earned because of the numerous false doctrines it teaches:

1. Biblical heretics *choose* their own "self-willed opinion" concerning what Scripture means. They choose to *not* honor the Holy Spirit inspired Scripture. They contrive their own inspiration (revelation), and in doing this they reject the Holy Spirit of truth Who leads people to the real Jesus (John 15:26).

2. Their opinion *does not submit* to the power of truth and leads to division and the formation of sects. The false faith teachers have caused immense worldwide division and damage to the Body of Christ. The false teachers, false prophets, and their followers qualify as a "False Faith Sect," because they teach *their* own way according to *their* personal revelation of isolated Scriptures, and for teaching "another Jesus," and "a different gospel" (2 Corinthians 11:4).

3. Their erroneous doctrinal opinions are of *personal preference* to gain a "financial advantage" over the ignorant and greedy through misrepresentation of Jesus and what His redemptive work on the cross represents (2 Peter 2:3). This is done through preaching the "false prosperity gospel," and using other verses incorrectly to fleece money out of the ignorant, assuring them God will reward their steadfast faith.

We must have the love for Jesus and the courage to oppose all false gospels that reject the *only* Gospel. Christians are not called to ignore false teachings about Jesus that constitute a false gospel and keep people in sin. We are called to look after each other and defend the true faith. Paul stated this clearly in 2 Timothy 4:1-4.

There is no way the early Church would have allowed the worldwide false faith doctrines about Jesus to be accepted as "the rule of teaching" in Christianity. The false teachers and false prophets who proclaimed "another Jesus" would have been "branded as wolves" in sheep's clothing (Matthew 7:15-17; Acts 20:29). We, who claim the Name of the real Jesus, need to be like the early Christians who obeyed the Scriptures. We need to warn those not yet invaded by these evil doctrines, and call or write letters to those who are snared by these horrible false teachings and explain the truth (James 5:19-20).

Doctrinal Leaven

Before we look at the salvation issue, we will recap some main areas of concern in each chapter. This information will testify to the fact, that concerning true doctrine, Paul said "A little leaven leaveneth the whole lump" (Galatians 5:9). In this case, the leaven that continues to grow globally is the false faith doctrine presented in the previous 17 chapters, as will be shown:

Chapter 1 shows their way of misrepresenting Scriptures.

Chapter 2 reveals all are accountable for sound doctrine.

Chapter 3 exposes that not all sickness is from the devil.

Chapter 4 discloses an occult doctrinal connection.

Chapter 5 refutes "positive confession" used improperly.

Chapter 6 is a rebuttal of "Four steps for health and wealth."

Chapter 7 finds that quantum faith is unbiblical.

Chapter 8 divulges bizarre manifestations at Bethel Church.

Chapter 9 corrects their personal opinion of God-pleasing faith.

Chapter 10 exposes how they distort Scriptures for money.

Chapter 11 verifies that holy angels don't gather money for us.

Chapter 12 is a shocker, showing many unbiblical teachings.

Chapter 13 reveals Christ's physical death doesn't redeem us.

Chapter 14 is their new way of presenting and using His blood.

Chapter 15 shows they reject Matthew 8:17 in proper context.

Chapter 16 finds them rejecting the true biblical atonement.

Chapter 17 unveils their healing power is not always from God.

Look again at the summary of these 17 chapters which expose the sins of false doctrine. Almost two hundred pages have clearly revealed dozens of false faith teachings in these chapters. Has the truth set in? Specifically, the main teachings/beliefs of the false Worldwide Faith Movement were not ordained by, and are not anointed by the LORD God, because they contradict Scripture.

Over a year ago on the radio, I heard an author speak who wrote a book refuting numerous false faith doctrines. He labeled some as heretical and blasphemous, which is accurate. I was disappointed when I heard him say that he went to a Word-Faith conference and met two nice ladies who were following these teachings. He referred to them as sincere. One thing is obvious; they were *sincerely deceived* since they were still involved with false teachings. Godly sincerity is found in renouncing a false Jesus, honoring the Word of God in context, and following and worshipping the true Son of God.

Does Faith in a False Atonement Assure Salvation?

Various quotes were listed in earlier chapters from faith teachers showing *their* belief in what Christ's atonement represents. The false gospel commonly preached by the global Faith Movement proclaims, "Jesus died to remove the curse of the Law for our sins to be forgiven, and to guarantee physical healing and financial prosperity for all."[3] Thus, this false threefold redemption gospel is defined as follows:

> Jesus shed his blood and died on the cross to forgive our sins and guarantee physical healing and abundant prosperity for all. Therefore, it is known as "The Health and Wealth gospel."

Now compare this counterfeit gospel with the true Gospel Jesus told His disciples to preach after His resurrection:

> Thus it is written, and thus it behoved Christ to suffer, and to rise from the dead the third day: And that repentance and remission of sins should be preached in His Name among all nations, beginning at Jerusalem (Luke 24:46-47).

When giving final instructions on how to preach the Gospel to the Jews and Gentiles, Jesus mentions repentance and forgiveness. He does *not* mention guaranteed physical healing and financial prosperity as part of His Gospel message. Peter followed His instructions at Pentecost (Acts 2:36-39), as did others who preached the LORD'S Gospel throughout *The Book of Acts*.

Though faith teachers say the blood of Jesus forgives our sins, they preach "a different" blood atonement, one Jesus did not teach. They add (Proverbs 30:5-6) to what His blood represents and guarantees (healing and money). So how can a counterfeit blood atonement gospel with "another Jesus" save anyone? It can't, according to the God-inspired Scriptural teachings Paul recorded in Galatians 1:8-9. Jesus told Paul (Galatians 1:11-12) there is only one

Gospel capable of saving, and all other gospels are accursed gospels. False gospels are accursed because they *reject and change* the way God Almighty said His Gospel was to be taught.

Those who want to please God and have assurance of a heavenly eternity must bow down to the confirmation of the true Gospel, in order to be partakers of God's grace (Philippians 1:7). When you put faith in the *only* Gospel of salvation (Acts 4:12), you will be sealed with the Holy Spirit of promise (Ephesians 1:13). Are you honoring His Gospel and His blood properly?

Preaching any distortion about Christ's work on the cross is a sin. Matthew 7:21-23 projects shocking insight for all who continue to teach "another Jesus." Not everyone who calls Jesus "Lord" will enter the kingdom of heaven, and false faith preachers worldwide call Him Lord (but which Jesus?). Only the ones who do the will of Christ's Father will enter the kingdom of heaven (verse 21). The Father's will is believing in the *real* Jesus (John 6:29), and teaching truth (John 17:17) about His Son so our sins can be forgiven. We are not to teach false doctrine about His healing, money, and what Christ's *precious blood* atonement represents—this is a false gospel!

Those who *continue* to crucify the Son of God with false teachings are in long-term trouble if they don't repent. People can prophesy, cast out demons, do miracles in His Name (verse 22) and end up hearing, "I never knew you. Depart from Me, you who practice iniquity and lawlessness" (verse 23). False gospel believers *practice* doctrinal iniquity, and without repentance are not destined for Heaven. The snare of false doctrine holds people captive in a state of spiritual intoxication. Recovery (*ananēphō*) to spiritual soberness occurs only with God-granted repentance (2 Timothy 2:25-26). Jesus desires for us to be sanctified in the truth so we will be assured of being with Him in Heaven (John 17:3, 17).

Don't accuse me of judging the salvation of the multitudes in the false Worldwide Faith Movement. The Scriptures judge all. Of their personal free will, *some* have chosen to reject Christ's *only* Gospel of forgiveness (Luke 24:45-48; Acts 2:38; 1 Corinthians 15:1-4). Misled individuals have placed their faith in "another Jesus" and "another gospel." By doing this, they have rejected the true Gospel and brought judgment into their lives from the Lord Jesus.

Sometimes Word-Faith believers say that "No weapon formed against them shall prosper." They are wrong. The weapons of many false doctrines have prospered against them by deceiving them into believing and teaching falsely about the real Jesus, His atonement, and various Bible topics. They talk about breaking curses. Yet they preach false doctrines, and warn people that false doctrines will bring a curse into your life. If this is true, some of them must have curses from false doctrines and darts from the evil one (Ephesians 6:16).

Various international false faith promoters have allowed "the god of this world" to blind their minds. They have chosen to place their faith in a gospel that preaches a false Christ, rather than placing their faith in the light of the glorious Gospel of Christ (2 Corinthians 4:3-4). The revival they have preached and proclaimed for years is here, but it's a deceptive revival of false doctrine (2 Corinthians 11:13-15). Scripture proves Word of Faith televangelists are misleading millions.

Will You Leave a Love Legacy When You Die?

Another major problem within the Worldwide Faith Movement is that their emphatic focus and teaching is on faith, rather than love. Their books and messages prove this. It is a self-focused faith (faith idolatry) instead of a Jesus-focused faith (Hebrews 12:2). Our focus should be on submission to the real Jesus, and serving Him with love as our focus. Too much emphasis on faith can cause one to be more concerned about faith, rather than love. Focusing on faith power breeds worldly arrogance (look at what *my* faith does), sounds like a noisy gong, clangs like a cymbal, and is irritating (1 Corinthians 13:1-2). Love power from Jesus edifies, blesses, and comforts (verse 13).

Jesus never commanded His disciples to be miracle workers. He commanded us to love one another as He loved us (John 13:34-35). When love dominates our relationship with Jesus, we can see our sins easily and receive quick correction with joy (Proverbs 12:1; 3 John 4). Love went to the cross at Calvary (Luke 23:33) so we could be forgiven (Luke 24:47). Love was resurrected and appeared with many infallible proofs to various people (Acts 1:1-3). Love sits on the throne, rules the universe, and upholds all things by Word of His power (Hebrews 1:3). Love will come for us one day and we will rejoice with Him in Heaven forever (John 14:1-3). Instead of asking the LORD to increase our faith only, we should be asking Him daily to *increase our love* to be greater than our faith.

Supposedly, in the last 50 years we have seen a tongues revival, a healing revival, a prophecy revival, a demonic deliverance revival, a miracle revival, and a faith revival. Can you see what is missing? We need a love *and* truth revival; one showing Jesus we love Him by serving Him and honoring His Word in proper context. This means eliminating all areas of sin in our lives and gathering together in love to minister to the needs of fellow Christians (Acts 2:42-47). With love, faith, and truth, we will be ongoing overcomers (1 John 5:4).

We cannot deny the fact that successful Christianity is sometimes painful in a variety of ways (2 Corinthians 6:4-10). Jesus showed us the way to live during His ministry. His way was *daily* submission and obedience to His Father (Hebrews 5:7-8). If we are to lead people to Heaven, we must continually conform to His Holy image and work at being less involved with the world, and more involved with Him and the Bible. Let's shine for Jesus (Daniel 12:3).

If you still need to repent concerning any of the false teachings that were exposed and refuted, *please* repent. Confess your sins of believing and following false doctrine, as well as teaching false doctrine to others. Destroy *all* items you have that promote false teachings like the obedient Christians did in Acts 19:18-20.

Finally, may the true Lord Jesus bless you with abundant love, discernment, peace, truth, and keep evil from deceiving you; may the LORD make His face to shine upon you and be gracious to you. Remember to work continually on your legacy of love and truth for the glory of the LORD, as you conform to the image of the real Jesus.

The time is short and the days are increasing with worldwide evil (Ephesians 5:15-17). Lead as many as possible to the LORD'S love and forgiveness (Jude 21-23).

Will I see you in Heaven?

Answer this question by looking at 2 Corinthians 13:5. Do you pass the test? Is the true Jesus in you? Do you need to renounce *any* false Jesus being preached by the Worldwide Faith Movement, who can't forgive your sins? If so, confess your sins now. Then receive (John 1:12) and confess the "real Jesus" as your Lord and Savior (Romans 10:9-10), and rejoice in His everlasting love and forgiveness.

Your name: _____

Endnotes:

1. W. E. Vine, *An Expository Dictionary of New Testament Words* (Old Tappan, New Jersey: Fleming H. Revell Company, 1966), p. 262.
2. Ibid., Vol. II, E-Li, p. 217.
3. Kenneth E. Hagin, *Redeemed From Poverty, Sickness, and Spiritual Death* (Tulsa, OK: Kenneth Hagin Ministries, 1983), pp. 1-2.

Author's Testimony of Physical Healing

My instant, miraculous healing happened around 1980. I was at the Raintree Racquetball Club playing racquetball with a friend. We had been playing hard for less than an hour when I moved quickly to my left to hit a backhand shot.

As I bent over and extended quickly, pain ripped through my lower right calf area. It felt like someone had hit me with a stick below my calf. I collapsed on the floor yelling in pain. Focusing on the injured area, I saw how my right calf muscle had pulled up under the lower calf. I had torn my Achilles tendon. Swelling was evident within a few minutes. The ugly gap where the tear occurred below my calf was the width of my forefinger.

Two kind friends carried me out to my van so I could drive to my apartment (I used my left leg). When I was being carried out, several club members saw my serious injury. During the drive to my apartment, I was wondering about finding an orthopedic surgeon to reattach my Achilles tendon to my calf.

When I reached my apartment, I called a friend who knew several doctors. I told him what had happened and asked him for the name of a Christian orthopedic surgeon. Before giving me any name, he prayed for me. The thought came into my mind to slowly touch my toe to the floor. As my toe touched the floor I felt a surge of warmth and energy flow from the back of my knee to my heel. *Instantly* my foot was flat on the floor and my Achilles tendon was reattached to my lower calf area.

I was amazed at His instant grace and mercy, and spent time in prayer thanking Him. To show what the Lord had done, I got in my van and drove back to the club where I had been carried out about an hour earlier. What happened next took place over thirty years ago, but it is still clear in my mind, as if it happened last week.

As I walked into the health club, some people who saw me carried out were seated in the dining area. One person said, "Did you already get your leg set in a cast?" I lifted up the warm-up pant on my right leg to show him and many other people seated that there was no cast on my leg. I looked at all the people and boldly said, "Just as my Achilles tendon was separated from my calf and is now reattached, your relationship with God is separated because of your sin. Jesus healed my ruptured Achilles and He will heal your relationship with God if you will ask Him to forgive your sins."

A Fresno State baseball player was sitting by himself and motioned for me to come over to him. He was Jewish and asked me to explain what I had just shared with everyone. He also wanted to know more about Jesus. I told him about Jesus as the Messiah, and how he could receive Jesus into his life and have his sins forgiven. He prayed and asked Jesus into his life as his Savior, and to receive forgiveness for his sins.

Suddenly, a staff person who had heard my testimony of how Jesus healed me asked to talk with me. He wanted to know how he could be sure if he was forgiven. I explained how *only* Jesus could forgive his sins so that he could get into heaven (Acts 4:12). A Christian employee covered for him at the front desk so he could go to the back room and receive Christ as his Lord and Savior. A few minutes later, he came out and told us he had prayed to have Jesus forgive his sins, and received Christ as his Savior.

In looking back, I see obvious reasons why God healed my ruptured Achilles: 1) A Jewish athlete gave his life to Messiah Jesus to have his sins forgiven. 2) A young student at Fresno State received Jesus to make sure he was forgiven and would go to heaven one day. 3) Several people saw me *carried* out of the club, and less than an hour later they saw me *walk* into the club. Thus, many heard about Jesus and His forgiveness. Word of my miraculous healing spread in the club, and it gave me more opportunities to share the Gospel.

There have been other times (for two years) I sought healing from the Lord to heal both of my hips, because the cartilage was completely worn down in the hip sockets. I believed *with faith* to be healed by God, but He said "No" to both hips, so I have artificial hips and faith that pleases Him.

I shared my instant physical healing to let you know that I have seen and experienced the supernatural work of the real Jesus, and I have seen a few (less than five) other instant physical healings in the last thirty years. I do believe in both instant and slow healings as directed by the Holy Spirit.

Also, I *definitely* believe in doctors for help and healing. Remember Luke, the beloved physician (Colossians 4:14), was also part of God's first century *will* in healing. We need prayer for healing, doctors for healing, each other's words of comfort and edification for healing, and we need to accept the LORD'S will in how healing transpires, if it does. Compared to spending eternity with Jesus in our glorified pain-free bodies (Revelation 21:4), our afflictions, though quite painful and limiting in some cases, are only momentary (2 Corinthians 4:17).

To make sure that I did not receive my healing from a healing demon, I have prayed sincerely to the LORD and said, "LORD, if this healing was demonic and it's not from You, I renounce it. I don't want it. Separate my Achilles tendon from my calf and I will find a Christian doctor for needed repairs." My healing has remained for over thirty years because the Lord Jesus did the healing. I am not ashamed of the Gospel or the gifts of healing that come from the Holy Spirit as God wills.

Friends have expressed concern about including my miraculous healing in this book, because those who don't believe in instant Holy Spirit healings might reject the book entirely. If you believe that God doesn't do any instant healings since the apostles died, *please* do not discard the important teachings and refutations found throughout this book. Warn those you know about the "eternal consequences" of placing faith in "another Jesus" and "another gospel."

As you have read through this book and learned from the Scriptures in proper context, I pray that you will remember the importance of abstaining from sin. If you do sin, be quick to repent. Cling to the real Jesus. We are one day closer to heaven. Have a good forever. I look forward to seeing you in our heavenly Paradise.

Sending love from Above to you,

Danny Frigulti

Daniel 12:3 … John 17:17

Bibliography

Bosworth, F. F. *Christ the Healer*. Grand Rapids, Michigan: Chosen Books, 2008.

Bruce, F. F. *The Spreading Flame*. Grand Rapids, Michigan: William B. Eerdmans Publishing Company, 1979.

Burns, Dr. Cathy. *Tongues, Prosperity, & Godhood*. Mt. Carmel: PA, Sharing, 2001.

Capps, Annette. *Quantum Faith*. England, Arkansas: Capps Publishing, 2010.

Capps, Charles. Capps, Annette. *Angels*. Tulsa, Oklahoma: Harrison House Inc., 1984.

Capps, Charles. *Authority in Three Worlds*. Tulsa, Oklahoma: Harrison House Inc., 1982.

Capps, Charles. *Faith and Confession*. England, Arkansas: Capps Publishing, 1987.

Capps, Charles & Annette. *God's Creative Power For Finances*. England, Arkansas: Capps Publishing, 2004.

Capps, Charles. *God's Creative Power For Healing.* England, AR: Capps Publishing, 1991.

Capps, Charles. *Releasing The Ability Of God Through Prayer.* England, Arkansas: Capps Publishing, 1978.

Capps, Charles. *The Tongue—A Creative Force.* England, AR: Capps Publishing, 1995.

Cho, Dr. David Yonggi. *The Fourth Dimension Volume One.* Alachua, Florida: Bridge-Logos, 1979.

Copeland, Gloria. *And Jesus Healed Them All.* Fort Worth, Texas: Kenneth Copeland Publications, 1981.

Copeland, Gloria, *God's Will is Prosperity.* Fort Worth, Texas: Kenneth Copeland Publications, 1978.

Copeland, Gloria. *The Protection Of Angels.* Fort Worth, Texas: Kenneth Copeland Publications, 1997.

Copeland, Kenneth. *Prosperity: The Choice Is Yours.* Fort Worth, Texas: Kenneth Copeland Publications, 1994.

Copeland, Kenneth. *The Force of Faith*. Fort Worth, Texas: Kenneth Copeland Publications, 1992.

Copeland, Kenneth. *The Laws of Prosperity*. Fort Worth, Texas: Kenneth Copeland Publications, 1974.

Copeland, Kenneth. *The Power Of The Tongue*. Fort Worth, Texas: Kenneth Copeland Publications, 1980.

Copeland, Kenneth. *You Are Healed!* Fort Worth, Texas: Kenneth Copeland Publications, 1979.

Dollar, Dr. Creflo A. *How To Obtain Healing*. College Park, Georgia: Creflo Dollar Ministries, 1999.

Dollar, Dr. Creflo A. *The Image Of Righteousness. You're More Than You Know*. Tulsa, OK: Harrison House, Inc., 2002.

Duplantis, Jesse. *Heaven—Close Encounters of the God Kind*. Tulsa, OK: Harrison House Inc., 1996.

Fisher, Ann. *Omni—Cosmics: Miracle Power Beyond the Subconscious*. West Nyack, New York: Parker Publishing Company, 1979.

Fisher, G. Richard and Goedelman, M. Kurt. *The Confusing World of Benny Hinn*. Saint Louis, Missouri: Personal Freedom Outreach, 2002.

Franklin, Judy & Davis, Ellyn. *The Physics Of Heaven*. Crossville, TN: Double Portion Publishing, 2012.

Gibson, Keith. *Wandering Stars*. Birmingham, Alabama: Solid Ground Christian Books, 2011.

Gossett, Don & Kenyon, E. W. *The Power Of Your Words*. New Kensington, Pennsylvania: Whitaker House, 1981.

Hagee, John. *The Power Of The Prophetic Blessing*. Brentwood, Tennessee: Worthy Publishing, 2012.

Hagee, John. *The Power To Heal*. Dallas, Texas: Horticultural Printers, 1991.

Hagin, Kenneth E. *How God Taught Me About Prosperity*. Tulsa, Oklahoma: Kenneth Hagin Ministries, 1985.

Hagin, Kenneth E. *How to Keep Your Healing*. Tulsa, Oklahoma: Kenneth Hagin Ministries, 1980.

Hagin, Kenneth E. *How to Write Your Own Ticket With God*. Tulsa, OK: Kenneth Hagin Ministries, 1979.

Bibliography

Hagin, Kenneth E. *How You Can Be Led by the Spirit of God.* Tulsa, OK: Kenneth Hagin Ministries, 2006.

Hagin, Kenneth E. *Plead Your Case.* Tulsa, OK: Kenneth Hagin Ministries, 1979.

Hagin, Kenneth E. *Redeemed From Poverty, Sickness, and Spiritual Death.* Tulsa, OK: Kenneth Hagin Ministries, 1983.

Hagin, Kenneth E. *The Name of Jesus.* Tulsa, Oklahoma: Kenneth Hagin Ministries, 1989.

Hagin, Kenneth E. *"You Can Have What You Say!"* Tulsa, OK: Kenneth Hagin Ministries, 1979.

Hagin, Kenneth E. *Words.* Tulsa, OK: Kenneth Hagin Ministries, 1979.

Hagin, Kenneth W. *Seven Hindrances to Healing.* Tulsa, OK: Kenneth Hagin Ministries, 1980.

Hayes, Dr. Norvel. *Confession Brings Possession.* Tulsa, OK: Harrison House, Inc., 1993.

Hayes, Dr. Norvel. *Faith Has No Feelings.* Tulsa, OK: Harrison House Inc., 1997.

Hayes, Norvel. *What to Do for Healing.* Tulsa, OK: Harrison House Inc., 1981.

Hickey, Marilyn. *Your Pathway to Miracles.* New Kensington, PA: Whitaker House, 2011.

Hinn, Benny. *Good Morning Holy Spirit.* Nashville, TN: Thomas Nelson, Inc., 2004.

Hinn, Benny. *"Rise & Be Healed!"* Orlando, Florida: Celebration Publishers Inc., 1991.

Hinn, Benny. *The Blood.* Lake Mary, Florida: Charisma House Publishers, 2006.

Hinn, Benny. *The Anointing.* Nashville, TN: Thomas Nelson, Inc., 1997.

Hinn, Benny. *Welcome, Holy Spirit.* Nashville, TN: Thomas Nelson, Inc., 1995.

Huch, Larry. *The 7 Places Jesus Shed His Blood.* New Kensington, PA: Whitaker House, 2004.

Hunt, Dave & T. A. McMahon. *The Seduction Of Christianity, Spiritual Discernment In The Last Days.* Bend, OR: The Berean Call, 2013.

Jakes, T. D. *God Longs To Heal You*. Shippensburg, PA: Destiny Image Publishers, 1995.

Jones, Floyd Nolen. *Which Version Is The Bible?* Humboldt, Tennessee: KingsWord Press, 2014.

Kautzsch, E. edited and enlarged. Translated by A. E. Cowley. *Gesenius' Hebrew Grammar*. Mineola, NY: Dover Publications, Inc., 2006.

Keil, C. F. and Delitzsch, Franz. *Commentary on the Old Testament*, Volume 7, *Isaiah*, Part II. Grand Rapids, Michigan: William B. Eerdmans Publishing Company, 1978.

Keil, C. F. and Delitzsch, Franz. *Commentary on the Old Testament*, Volume 5, *Psalms, Fourth Book Of The Psalter*. Grand Rapids, Michigan: William B. Eerdmans Publishing Company, 1978.

Kenyon, E. W. *Identification*. Lynnwood, Washington: Kenyon's Gospel Publishing Society, 2012.

Kenyon, E. W. *Jesus the Healer*. Lynnwood, Washington: Kenyon's Gospel Publishing Society, 2010.

Kenyon, E. W. & Gossett, Don. *Speak Life*. New Kensington, PA: Whitaker House, 2013.

Kenyon, E. W. *The Hidden Man*. Lynnwood, Washington: Kenyon's Gospel Publishing Society, 1970.

Kenyon, E. W. *The Bible in the Light of Our Redemption*. Lynnwood, Washington: Kenyon's Gospel Publishing Society. 1995.

Kenyon, E. W. *What Happened from the Cross to the Throne*. Lynnwood, Washington: Kenyon's Gospel Publishing Society, 2010.

Lenski, R. C. H. *The Interpretation of St. Mark's Gospel*. Minneapolis, MN: Augsburg Publishing House, 1964.

Maldonado, Guillermo. *How To Walk In The Supernatural Power of God*. New Kensington, PA: Whitaker House, 2011.

Maldonado, Guillermo. *Jesus Heals Your Sickness Today!* Miami, Florida: *ERJ Publicaciones,* 2009.

Meyer, Joyce. *Be Healed In Jesus' Name*. New York, NY: Warner Faith Printing, 2000.

Meyer, Joyce. *Prepare to Prosper*. Tulsa, OK: Harrison House, Inc., 1997.

Meyer, Joyce. *The Most Important Decision You Will Ever Make*. New York, NY: Warner Faith Printing, 2003.

Bibliography

Mumford, Bob. *The Purpose of Temptation*. Old Tappan, New Jersey: Fleming H. Revell Company, 1973.

Osborn, T. L. *Healing the Sick A Living Classic*. Tulsa, OK: Harrison House, Inc., 1992.

Osborn, T. L. *One Hundred Divine Healing Facts*. Tulsa, OK: Harrison House, Inc., 1983.

Osteen, Dodie. *If My Heart Could Talk*. New York, NY: FaithWords, 2016.

Osteen, Joel. *I Declare 31 Promises To Speak Over Your Life*. New York, NY: FaithWords, 2013.

Osteen, Joel. *The Power of I Am Two Words That Will Change Your Life Today*. New York, NY: FaithWords, 2015.

Osteen, John. *There Is A Miracle In Your Mouth*. Houston, Texas: Lakewood Church, 1972.

Osteen, John. *Your Words Hold A Miracle*. New York, NY: FaithWords, 2012.

Parsley, Rod. *At The Cross Where Healing Begins*. Lake Mary, FL: Creation House Press, 2003.

Parsley, Rod. *The Double Portion Anointing*. Columbus, Ohio: Results Publishing, 2002.

Parsley, Rod. *Your Harvest is Come*. Columbus, Ohio: Results Publishing, 1999.

Price, Frederick K. C. *Is Healing for All?* Los Angeles, CA: Faith One Publishing, 2015.

Price, Frederick K. C. *The Power of Positive Confession*. Los Angeles, CA: Faith One Publishing, 1992.

Price, Frederick K. C. *Three Keys To Positive Confession*. Los Angeles, CA: Faith One Publishing, 1994.

Prince, Joseph. *Healing Promises*. Lake Mary, Florida: Charisma House, 2012.

Prince, Joseph. *Health And Wholeness Through The Holy Communion*. Printed in the United States of America, Fourth edition, thirty-fifth print: September 2015.

Roberts, Oral. *Miracle of Seed—Faith*. Old Tappan, New Jersey: Fleming H. Revell Company, 1970.

Robertson, A. T. *Word Pictures In The New Testament—The Gospels of Matthew and Mark*. Volume I, Nashville, Tennessee: Broadman Press, 1930.

Robertson, A. T. and Davis, W. Hersey. *A New Short Grammar of the Greek Testament*, 10th Edition. Grand Rapids, MI: Baker Book House, 1982.

Savelle, Jerry. *The Nature of Faith*. Crowley, TX: Jerry Savelle Ministries, 2009.

Savelle, Jerry. *Touch Not God's Anointed. The danger of Judging Other Ministers*. Crowley, TX: Jerry Savelle Ministries, 2012.

Savelle, Jerry. *What I Learned from the men who imparted to me the most*. Crowley, TX: Jerry Savelle Ministries, 2014.

Strong, James. *Strong's Exhaustive Concordance of the Bible*. Nashville, Tennessee: Abingdon Press, 1976.

Vine, W. E. *An Expository Dictionary of New Testament Words*. Old Tappan, New Jersey: Fleming H. Revell Company, 1966.

Webster's Encyclopedic Unabridged Dictionary of the English Language. New York, NY: Gramercy Books, 1996.

Winston, Bill. *The God Kind of Faith*. Oak Park, IL: Bill Winston Ministries, 2014.

Winston, Dr. Bill. *The Law of Confession*. Tulsa, OK: Harrison House Publishers, 2009.

Wommack, Andrew. *God Wants You Well*. Tulsa, OK: Harrison House Publishers 2010.

Made in the USA
Lexington, KY
20 June 2017